NOW THAT'S WHAT I CALL

A BIG FECKIN' IRISH BOOK

Murphy O'Dea

NOW THAT'S WHAT I CALL

A BIG FECKIN' IRISH BOOK

Murphy O'Dea

Jammers with
Insults ● Proverbs ● Family Names ● Trivia ● Slang

THE O'BRIEN PRESS
DUBLIN

Published 2011 by The O'Brien Press Ltd
12 Terenure Road East, Rathgar, Dublin 6, Ireland.
Tel: +353 1 4923333; Fax: +353 1 4922777
Email: books@obrien.ie; Website: www.obrien.ie
First published in this format 2010 by Fall River Press

This book contains portions of the previously published books
2nd *Feckin' Book of Irish Slang* (2006), *Feckin' Book of Irish Insults* (2006),
and *The Book of Feckin' Irish Trivia* (2009), all originally published by
The O'Brien Press Ltd., excluding the chapters Feckin' Irish Surnames
and Feckin' Irish Proverbs.

ISBN: 978-1-84717-251-8

A catalogue record for this title is available from The British Library

Text © 2006, 2009, 2010 by Colin Murphy
Illustrations © 2006, 2009, 2010 by Donal O'Dea

1 2 3 4 5 6
11 12 13 14

Printed and bound by ScandBook AB, Sweden
The paper used in this book is produced using pulp from managed forests.

The information in this book has been drawn from many sources and is
assumed to be accurate. Although every effort has been made to verify the
information, the publishers cannot guarantee its perfect accuracy.

contents

introduction

So you think just because your name is Kelly or O'Sullivan that you're Irish? You think because your grandfather came from County Cork you can wear the green with pride?

Well hold your horses there, bucko! Before anyone can claim to have genuine Irish green in their blood, they have to know their *doss artists* from their *doxies* and their *yokes* from their *yonks*. They must be able to insult someone with a neat turn of Irish word-smithing like, *"You have a face like the divil's arse!"* You'll need to know your Irish trivia—like the fact that hurling is the world's fastest field sport or that St. Brendan discovered America a thousand years before Columbus! And while you're at that, you'll definitely need a sprinkling of proverbial Irish wisdom such as *Is minic cuma aingeal ar an*

Diabhal féin, or in other words, "There is often the look of an angel on the Devil himself." And to round it all off, if you've got a common Irish name, you absolutely need to know where you and yours originated, your family motto, what your name means, and all that oul' blarney.

Which is why this book is a must for every aspiring Irish person. This new volume is crammed with tons of Irish slang, is jammers with Irish insults and proverbs, has a gansey-load of fascinating facts and general Irish trivia, and features an illuminating explanation of the origins of the twenty-five most popular Irish surnames in history. In short, it has all the craic a self-respecting Irish mucksavage could ever need! Get reading or you'll be in rag order!

feckin'
irish
slang

Stop the lights! Here's all the Irish slang you've been gummin' for. Whether you're a chancer or a doss artist; a heifer or a nice bit of talent; this latest collection of slang is definitely worth a dekko. It's been yonks in the making and has a rake of words and expressions that are absolutely mingin'.

It might give a beamer to a bishop but it's guaranteed to put a savage smile on your puss even if you're scuttered. So what are you waiting for, it would be a mortaller to miss out.

Afters (n)

Dessert.

(USAGE) *"I had a batter-burger and chips for the main course and a flagon of cider for afters."*

Alco (n)

Person who is regularly inebriated.

(USAGE) *"Just because I've been injecting vodka into my oranges doesn't make me an alco."*

Amadán (n)

Idiot. Imbecile. Fool.

(USAGE) *"Yes, Your Honour, I arrested the amadán as he attempted to burgle the Garda station."*

Any use? (expr)

Was it any good?

(USAGE) *"Is he any use in bed since he got dem Viagra on the Internet?"*

Apache (n)

A joyrider.

(USAGE) *"That smart-arsed little apache fecker calls himself 'Dances with Porsches.'"*

RIGHT, MY LITTLE APACHE FECKER. PREPARE TO BE SCALPED!

Arra be whist (expr)

Be quiet. Shut up.

(USAGE) *"Arra, be whist worrying, doctor. Sure haven't I cut down to sixty fags a day?"*

Article (n) (derog)

A person.

(USAGE) *"Our English teacher is a drunken old lech. In fact, he's a definite article."*

Babby (n)

Baby. Small child.

(USAGE) *"Me Ma had her first babby when she was fifteen. So I thought I'd keep the family tradition goin'."*

Banjaxed (adj) (*see also* Knackered)

Broken. Severely damaged.

(USAGE) *"Me marriage to Deco is completely banjaxed."*

Beamer (n)

When one's face goes red with embarrassment.

(USAGE) *"I had a right beamer on me when me top came off in the pool."*

Begorrah (expr)

By God!

(USAGE) US actor 1: *"Begorrah, me lad, 'tis a fine soft mornin' to be sure."*

US actor 2: *"'Tis, to be sure, to be sure, begorrah and bejapers."*

Irish actor: *"Excuse me while I throw up."*

Note: This word does not exist outside Hollywood movies.

Bejapers (expr)

By Jesus!

(USAGE) US actor 1: *"Bejapers, Mickeen, I've lost me shillelagh!"*
US actor 2: *"Begorrah, Pat, maybe the fairies stole it."*
Irish actor: *"If you don't shut up I'm going to stab you in the eye with a pencil."*

B. L. O. (expr)

Be look-out. Keep watch.

(USAGE) *"Hey, Mick! B.L.O. while I hook the foreman's car bumper to this crane."*

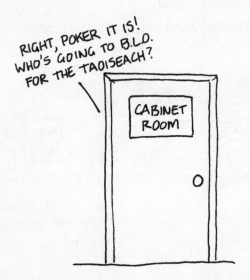

RIGHT, POKER IT IS! WHO'S GOING TO B.L.O. FOR THE TAOISEACH?

CABINET ROOM

Belt (n) (v)

A thump with the fist. To strike.

(USAGE) *"Me mot gave me a belt just because I told her I'd slept with her Ma."*

Black (adj)

Extremely crowded.

(USAGE) *"Deadly, Anto! This place is black with women. Funny name though, The Lesbar."*

Black Maria (n)

Garda van (patrol vehicle).

(USAGE) *"The Black Maria was full of planning officials."*

Black Stuff (n)

Stout.

(USAGE) *"Nine pints of the black stuff and a gin and tonic for me mot, please."*

Blather (n) (v)

Empty, worthless talk.

(USAGE) *"What are ye blatherin' on about, Taoiseach?"*

BLATHER... BLATHER...

BLATHER... BLATHER...

Bog (1) (n)

Rural Ireland.

(USAGE) Dub 1: *"Y'know, down de bog dey've never heard of curry chips."*

Dub 2: *"Jaysus. So dey're not sophisticated like us?"*

Bog (2) (n)

The toilet.

(USAGE) *"Great. You might have told me your bog's out of order before you served me the vindaloo and seven lagers."*

Brickin' it (v)

Extremely nervous or scared.

(USAGE) *"I've been brickin' it ever since I used her green party dress to make a flag for the Ireland match."*

Bucko (n) (derog)

Unsavoury or untrustworthy youth.

(USAGE) *Garda: "Y'know sarge, I suspect that fella standing on that poor oul wan's head is a bit of a bucko."*

Business, the (n)

Something cool.

(USAGE) *"The sporty lights on me new car are the business!"*

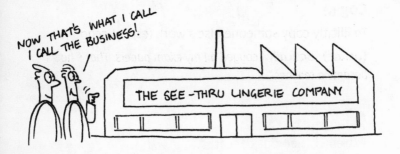

NOW THAT'S WHAT I CALL I CALL THE BUSINESS!

THE SEE-THRU LINGERIE COMPANY

Cacks (n)

Underwear (esp. male).

(USAGE) *"Me boyfriend changes his cacks so little that he doesn't have to drop them, he just hits them and they shatter."*

Cat (adj)

Terrible. Useless.

(USAGE) *"My guard dog is cat."*

Chancer (n)

Untrustworthy person.

(USAGE) *"The Minister for Justice is a right chancer."*

Cog (v)

To illicitly copy someone else's work (esp. at school).

(USAGE) *"Basically I cogged all my exam papers. That's how I became a teacher."*

Cop on (v)

Get wise. Don't be so stupid.

(USAGE) *"Those Irish Times guys need to cop on."*

The Irish Times

What's Hot

- A trendy overpriced bistro in D4 that's around the corner from my apartment.

- A gizmo mummy bought me for €1,736. Don't know what it does but it looks so cool.

- Exotic objets d'art that look vaguely phallic. (Hey, can I keep this?)

- Recommending obscure charities to appear socially conscious but still cool.

- Not working 'cause Daddy's so rich.

What's Cold

- *The Irish Times'* "What's Hot, What's Cold" column.

- Self-appointed arbiters of style who don't know their arse from their elbow.

- Ice, snow, northern winds.

Craic (n) (*Pronunciation:* crack)

Fun.

(USAGE) *"There's great craic to be found in that pub on the corner."*

Note: Misinterpretation of this expression has led to several arrests of foreign visitors who were caught trying to purchase a particular illicit drug.

Cute hoor (n)

Suspiciously resourceful gentleman.

(USAGE) *Speaking from his yacht off Bermuda, the cute hoor denied he'd made any payments to politicians in return for favourable building contracts.*

Dander (n)

Lazy stroll.

(USAGE) *"Hey, Mary, can we hurry this dander to the pub up a bit?"*

Deadner (n)

To punch someone sharply at the top of the arm.

(USAGE) *"Hey, Damo, let's give that guy with his arm in a sling a deadner!"*

Dekko (n)

A look at. An inspection.

(USAGE) *"Jaysus! Have a dekko at the shape of yer woman's arse!"*

YEAH, I'LL BE RIGHT THERE MARY
I'M JUST HAVING A DEKKO AT THE
LOCAL, EH, WILDLIFE.

Doing a line (expr)

Courting. Going out steadily with someone.

(USAGE) *"So I asked her if she fancied doing a line with me and she tells me to feck off and get my own cocaine."*

Doss artist (n)

Layabout who draws the dole despite availability of work.

(USAGE) *"My husband used to do the odd bit of painting. Now he's just a doss artist."*

DOSS ARTIST UNKNOWN

Doxie (n)

Dockland prostitute.

(USAGE) *"The legs on that doxie, Shay . . . I think me ship's just come in!"*

Elephants (adj)

Extremely drunk.

(USAGE) *"Those two old cows at the bar are elephants."*

Fag (n)

Cigarette.

(USAGE) *"Aaah, Jaysus, Trish. I know I'm not that good in bed, but couldn't you wait until I'm finished before you have your fag?"*

Feck (v) (n)

Politically correct term for f*ck.

(USAGE) *"Ah, feck off Father Murphy. You're nothing but a feckin' fecker."*

OH FECK, I SAID F*CK!!!

Flaming (adj)

Extremely drunk.

(USAGE) *"She was so flamin' she went out like a light."*

Flicks (n)

Cinema.

(USAGE) Girl 1: *"Was it a sad ending at the flicks last night?"*
Girl 2: *"Yeah. I ended up pregnant."*

Flute (n)

Male sexual organ.

(USAGE) *"My boyfriend doesn't so much have a flute as a tin whistle."*

Gameball (expr)

Great. Excellent. I agree. Okay.

(USAGE) *"At the end of camogie matches the girls are going to swap their shirts? Gameball!"*

Gansey (n)

Jumper. Sweater. Pullover.

(USAGE) *"I'd love to be inside her gansey on a cold day like this."*

Gansey-load (adj)

(*see also* Rake of)

Many. Lots. An excess.

(USAGE) *"There's a gansey-load of dossers in the Dáil."*

NOW THAT'S WHAT I CALL A GANSEY-LOAD!

Geebag (n)

Woman of unpleasant character.

(USAGE) *"Me wife's a right geebag."*

Gee-Eyed (adj)

Having partaken of a large quantity of ale and/or spirits.

(E.G.) *Subject was so inebriated that his eyes have shifted from the normal horizontal orientation.*

Gift (adj)

Expression of pleasant surprise.

(USAGE) *"So they're going to put all of Ireland's estate agents in a ship and sink it in the Atlantic? Gift!"*

Gingernut (n)

Redheaded man or woman.

(USAGE) *"I've always wondered, Edna, do gingernuts like you just have red hair on your head or . . . Ow! Jaysus, me eye!"*

Git (n)

Contemptible male.

(USAGE) *'You stupid git! You puked in me pocket!'*

OUR NEW APPRENTICES WILL BE KNOWN AS GENERAL INSURANCE TRAINEES. OR G.I.T.s FOR SHORT

IRISH INSURANCE LTD.

Give out (v)

Nag or criticise someone.

(USAGE) *"The minister finally gave out to the British Government after Sellafield exploded and wiped out the east coast of Ireland."*

Go (n)

A fight.

(USAGE) *"Yes, Your Honour, I did have a go at him. Then Knuckler had a go, then Mauler had a go, then Crusher Molloy had a go, then . . ."*

Gob (1) (n)

Mouth.

(USAGE) *"I wish the Minister for Justice would keep his gob shut."*

Gob (2) (v)

To expectorate forcefully.

(USAGE) *"So I hear you gobbed the P.E. teacher in the ear, headmaster?"*

THAT'S WHAT I CALL "GOB" OF THE SEASON

Gobshite (n)

Person of below average IQ. Socially inept individual.

(USAGE) *"The Minister for Finance is a complete gobshite."*

Gossoon (n)

Small child.

(USAGE) *"I'll have to stop leaving me little gossoon with me husband. His first words were: 'Jaysus, I've a pain in me bollox'."*

Go way outta that! (expr)

I don't believe it!

(USAGE) *"You were seen in casualty after only three days? Go way outta that!"*

Grand (adj)

Good. Fine.

(USAGE) Government Minister: *"Ripping off people is grand with us!"*

Gullier (n)

In the game of marbles, the largest.

(USAGE) *"Hey, mister, can I borrow your glass eye to use as a gullier?"*

Gummin' (v)

Dying for. Can't wait for.

(USAGE) *"Yer wan with the false teeth is gummin' for a snog."*

Hardchaw (n)

Tough guy, easily provoked.

(USAGE) *"He's such a hardchaw he opens his beer bottles with his nostril."*

Hash (n)

Mess. Foul-up.

(USAGE) *"He made a hash of rolling the hash."*

Heavin' (adj)

Thoroughly packed.

(USAGE) *"In the planning trial the defendant's box was heavin' with county councillors."*

Heifer (adj)

A very unattractive girl.

(USAGE) *"She may be a feckin' heifer, but she's got a great set of udders."*

AND DO YOU, MICK, TAKE THIS HEIFER... SORRY... HEATHER TO BE YOUR LAWFUL WEDDED...

Holliers (n)

Holidays. Vacation.

(USAGE) Girl 1: *"So I hear you and Mick never left your room your entire holliers . . . ?"* (giggle)
Girl 2: *"Yeah. The gobshite was langered for two weeks."*

Holy Joe (n)

Self-righteous, sanctimonious hypocrite.

(USAGE) *"If Holy Joes are so holy, how come there's always so many of them queuing for confession?"*

Hoof (1) (v)

To walk hurriedly.

(USAGE) *"The judge hoofed it out of the massage parlour when the Guards arrived."*

WE'LL RECONVENE IN THE MORNING!

Hoof (2) (v)

To kick a ball very hard and high.

(USAGE) *"He's great at hoofing the ball over the bar. Just a shame we're playing soccer."*

Horrors (n)

Bad hangover.

(USAGE) *"I'm really in the horrors this morning. I think that fifteenth pint must have been bad."*

Hump, the (n)

In a sulk.

(USAGE) *"He got in a hump 'cause I wouldn't give him a hump."*

Jack/Jackeen (n)

Dubliner.

(USAGE) *"Tradesmen in Dublin are so shite they're called jacks of all trades."*

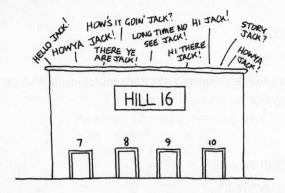

Jacked (adj)

Exhausted.

(USAGE) Solicitor: *"I'm jacked from counting all the money I've made from Tribunals."*

Jack-in-the-box (n)

Dead Dubliner.

(USAGE) *"Here lies a jack-in-the-box. He lived, he littered, he died."*

Jaded (adj)

Very tired.

(USAGE) Biddy: *"You look jaded. Did you sleep with Mick?"*
Clare: *"Well, we didn't exactly do much sleeping."*

Japers (expr)

Wow!

(USAGE) Nurse 1: *"Japers, sister, the suppository for that man was very big!"*
Nurse 2: *"Hey, has anyone seen my thermos?"*

Knackered (adj)

Extremely tired.

(USAGE) Supermarket manager: *"I'll never get knackered ripping Irish people off."*

Knick-knacking (expr)

Ringing a doorbell and then hiding.

(USAGE) *"The British Ambassador was caught knick-knacking at the French Embassy."*

Lady Muck (n)

Self-important, stuck-up woman.

(USAGE) *"She's a right Lady Muck, havin' a gin and tonic with her chips!"*

LADIES AND GENTLEMEN. THE RIGHT HONOURABLE LORD AND LADY MUCK.

Lamp out of (v)

To hit someone very hard.

(USAGE) Garda: *"Well, the guy was marching for world peace, so naturally I lamped him out of it."*

Legger (n)

A rapid exit from a situation.

(USAGE) *"The milkman had to do a legger when me husband came home."*

Let on (v)

To pretend.

(USAGE) *"No, you don't have a brain tumour, Mr. Hogan, I was only letting on."*

HE SAID HE WAS GOING TO GET HIS PENIS ENLARGED, BUT I'M SURE HE WAS ONLY LETTING ON.

Life of Reilly (expr)

Living a carefree existence.

(USAGE) *"Being responsible for Ireland's health service is the life of Reilly!"*

Locked (adj)

A state of total inebriation.

(USAGE) *"I was locked in the pub all night."*

Loopers (adj)

Crazy.

(USAGE) *"It's loopers what psychiatrists charge."*

Lose the head (v)

Lose one's temper.

(USAGE) *"She kicked him in the face and he lost the head."*

Mess, to (v)

To fool about.

(USAGE) *"I wasn't messin', Angela. I really do want to get your bra off."*

THEY'RE A RIGHT PAIR OF MESSERS OKAY.

MESSRS MORAN + HOGAN SOLICITORS

Messages (n)

Shopping.

(USAGE) *"I need to get a few messages—beer, stout, whiskey, and five packs of fags."*

Mickey (n)

Childish name for male organ.

(USAGE) *"When he sees a short skirt, his mickey's like a divining rod."*

Mind your house! (expr)

In team sports, a warning of a tackle from behind.

(USAGE) *"Mind your house, Anto! There's a bleedin' bulldozer about to demolish it!"*

VROM...
VROOOM!

Mortaller (n)

A mortal sin.

(USAGE) *"The price of car insurance in Ireland is a mortaller."*

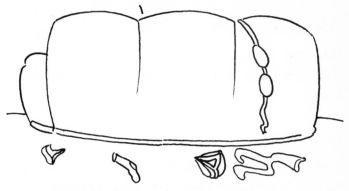

COURSE IT'S NOT A MORTALLER, DEIRDRE.
SURE I'D KNOW. I'M A BISHOP.

Mot (n)

Girlfriend.

(USAGE) *"Me mot drinks tequila sunrises like there's no tomorrow."*

Mucksavage (n)

Country fellow lacking in sophistication.

(USAGE) *"No, you big mucksavage, you may not eat curry chips in the delivery room."*

Nippy (1) (adj)

Cold.

(USAGE) *"Her arse must be a bit nippy wearing that skirt."*

Nippy (2) (adj)

Fast. Agile.

(USAGE) *"Her arse must be a bit nippy wearing that skirt."*

Off one's face (expr)

Very drunk.

(USAGE) *"I was so off my face that I landed on my face."*

On the lash (expr)

A prolonged drinking session.

(USAGE) Solicitor: *"I ripped off so many people this week I could go on the lash for the rest of my natural life."*

On the piss (expr)

A prolonged drinking session.

(USAGE) *"I'm sick of this Dáil debate on the Health Service. Let's go on the piss, Minister."*

Oul' wan (n)

Mother.

(USAGE) *"Me oul' wan had me when she was sixteen."*

Pain in the hole (expr)

Someone or something very irritating.

(USAGE) *"People from Dublin are a pain in the hole."*

THIS NEW RECTAL PROBE IS DESIGNED TO CURE PAINS IN THE HOLE.

Pelting (adj)

Raining heavily.

(USAGE) *"The forecast said sunny weather, so it's bound to be pelting."*

Perishing (adj)

Extremely cold.

(USAGE) *"Me and Anto were perishin' havin' sex under the bus shelter."*

Petrified drunk (adj)

Completely intoxicated.

(USAGE) *"Y'know Trish, it's ironic that when he's petrified drunk there's one part of him that never goes stiff."*

Pile of shite (expr)

Something utterly useless or terrible.

(USAGE) *"The manure I had delivered was a pile of shite."*

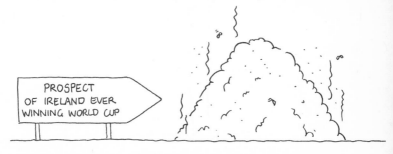

PROSPECT OF IRELAND EVER WINNING WORLD CUP

Plankin' it (v)

To be extremely nervous or scared.

(USAGE) *"She's been plankin' it ever since Mick's Celtic shirt came out of the wash dark blue."*

Póg (n)

Kiss.

(USAGE) *"Well, it started off as a little póg on the cheek. I'm due in September."*

Powerful (adj)

Brilliant. Fantastic.

(USAGE) *"The power in Robbo's new car is powerful."*

Puck (n)

Punch.

(USAGE) *"My dentist ripped me off so much I gave him a puck in the teeth."*

Puss (n)

Sulky face.

(USAGE) *"He had a puss on him just because I drove the car through the livingroom window."*

Quare (1) (adj)

Odd.

(USAGE) *"Isn't it a quare thing how stamp duty in Ireland is ten times more expensive than everywhere else on the planet?"*

IT'S VERY QUARE HOW WOMEN NEVER FOUND ME ATTRACTIVE BEFORE I WON THE LOTTO?

Quare (2) (adj)
Great.

(USAGE) *"That comedian from Cork is a quare fella."*

Rag order (adj)
Unkempt. In disarray.

(USAGE) *"Me knickers are in rag order."*

Rake (adj)
A great many.

(USAGE) *"The garden centre sold a rake of rakes last Saturday."*

Rasher (n)

Slice of bacon (esp. streaky).

(USAGE) *"Of course I'm looking after meself, Ma. I eat six rasher sandwiches every night after me eight pints of lager."*

Redser (n)

A person with red hair.

(USAGE) *"His mot's a redser with beautiful hair that goes right down her back. Unfortunately she's got none on her head."*

Root, to (1) (v)

To search for.

(USAGE) *"I was having a root for her bra fastener when she gave me a root in the nuts."*

Root, to (2) (v)

To kick forcefully.

(USAGE) *"He was taking so long to find my bra fastener I gave him a root in the nuts."*

Ructions (n)

Loud verbal commotion.

(USAGE) *"There were ructions in the county council when their junket to the Bahamas was cancelled."*

Sambo (n)

A sandwich.

(USAGE) *"You can't beat an egg, bacon, sausage, and black pudding sambo for a bit a classy nosh, eh, Taoiseach?"*

Savage (adj)

Great. Tremendous.

(USAGE) *"Twelve pints followed by a large chips and double batterburger is absolutely savage."*

Scanger (n)

Female lacking in sophistication.

(USAGE) *"The scanger drank her finger bowl."*

Feckin' Irish Slang

Scelped (adj)

Person who's got a very short haircut.

(USAGE) *"Jaysus, Trish, see how they scelped ye down below for the operation? It makes ye look years younger!"*

Scran (n)

Food.

(USAGE) *"The fat-arsed cow eats more scran than a horse."*

Scratcher (n)

Bed.

(USAGE) *"If you're not out of the scratcher and here in ten minutes operating on this man's brain, you're fired."*

Scuttered (adj)

Inebriated.

(USAGE) *"I was so scuttered that the estate agent started to sound honest."*

PISSED   SCUTTERED

Session (n)

A prolonged drinking bout.

(USAGE) *"The cabinet regularly holds emergency sessions."*

Shaper (n)

Person who walks with exaggerated strut to effect "coolness."

(USAGE) *"He was such a shaper that when he walked up to me he gave me a black eye with the back of his knee."*

Shitting bricks (adj)

Extremely fearful.

(USAGE) *"I'm shittin' bricks the doctor'll tell me I've got acute diarrhoea."*

Sketch! (expr)

Used in school to indicate approach of a teacher.

(USAGE) *"Sketch! Quick Mick, better take yer boot off little Johnny's head."*

Slapper (n)

Female of low morals and poor taste in clothing.

(USAGE) *"You're not really going to make that slapper a minister, are you, Taoiseach?"*

Sloshed (adj)

Totally drunk.

(USAGE) *"I was so sloshed I actually believed a solicitor."*

Snapper (n)

Baby.

(USAGE) *"If he wants to have one more snapper I swear I'm going to snap the bleedin' thing off."*

Sound (adj)

Good. Solid. Dependable.

(USAGE) *"That ventriloquist is a sound fella."*

Spud (1) (n)

Potato.

(USAGE) *"She has a head like a raw spud."*

Spud (2) (expr)
Nickname for anyone with the surname Murphy.

(USAGE) *"Yer man Spud has a head like a raw spud."*

Steamboats (adj)
Completely intoxicated.

(USAGE) *"The two old battleships at the bar are steamboats."*

Stop the lights! (expr)
What! I don't believe it!

(USAGE) *"A non-corrupt planning official? Stop the lights!"*

Taig (n)
Northern Irish term for a Catholic.

(USAGE) *"The Vatican is full of Taigs."*

Tip (n)

Messy establishment or room.

(USAGE) *"The bedroom was a complete tip after the chip fight."*

Togs (n)

Swimming shorts.

(USAGE) *"Jackie's togs have the same amount of material as a hanky."*

Trick-act, to (v)

To mess about, to indulge in horseplay.

(USAGE) *"I was just trick-acting with Deirdre and hey presto, she's bleedin' pregnant."*

Wear, to (v)

To engage in a prolonged passionate kiss.

(USAGE) *"Me an' Anto just started wearin' and before I knew it we weren't wearin' anything."*

WHAT WILL I WEAR AT THE PARTY TONIGHT?

ME?

Wojus (adj)

Extremely poor quality.

(USAGE) *"Every bleedin' government service in Ireland is wojus."*

Yoke (1) (n)

Any object.

(USAGE) *"Anto's got a lovely yoke."*

Yoke (2) (n)

Derogatory term for person of uncertain character (esp. female).

(USAGE) *"The paralytic one swinging her bra over her head is a right yoke."*

Yonks (n)

A very long time.

(USAGE) *"It'll be yonks upon yonks before Ireland wins the World Cup."*

Youngwan (n)

Female youth.

(USAGE) *"Hey you, youngfellas, here's youngwans!"*

Zeds (n)

Sleep.

(USAGE) *"I caught a few zeds last night while Mick was making love to me."*

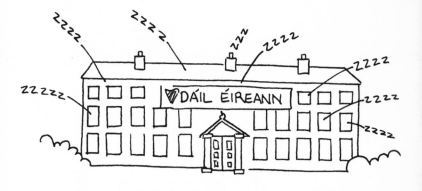

feckin'
irish
insults

ey you! You with the face like a constipated greyhound! You with the arse that's the width of a Mullingar heifer! I hear you're the sap in the family tree and they say you'd wring drink from a floozy's knickers.

But why stand there and be insulted? With the help of this invaluable collection of tried and tested Irish insults you can happily tell your boss that for someone with no cows he produces an awful lot of bullshit. Or your husband that he's so boring he couldn't entertain an idea. Or your wife that she has a face like the back of a turf cart! So get stuck in and be sure to get your insult in first!

Any friend of yours is a friend of yours.
You are a gobshite, as is anyone associated with you.

As fat as a Galway bishop.
Overweight. (Possibly conceived with the generously proportioned and amorous Bishop Casey in mind.)

**A sharp tongue doesn't mean
she has a keen mind.**

She's a stupid bitch.

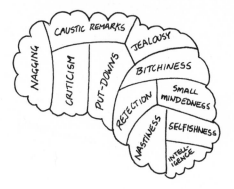

**Asking her who's the father would be like
asking which bean caused the fart.**

She's of loose virtue.

JAYSUS, JACINTA, HE'S THE IMAGE OF TOM, DICK AND HARRY.

As tight as a nun's knickers.
He's a stingy bastard.

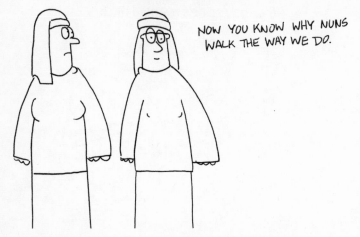

As useful as a chocolate teapot.
Utterly useless.

As useful as an ashtray in a force-10 gale.
Absolutely useless.

As useful as a one-legged man in an arse-kicking contest.
Totally useless.

For someone without any cows, he produces an awful lot of bullshit.

All talk, no substance.

God used him as the blueprint for a gobshite.

He is the mother of all gobshites.

Go on home and tell your oul' wan to get married.

You're a bastard.

He cheats when filling out opinion polls.

He is a moron of the first degree.

He couldn't hit sand if he fell off a camel.
His aim is brutal.

He couldn't pick the winner of a one-horse race.
His judgment is utterly crap.

He'd live in your left ear and grow spuds in your right.

He's a stingy gobshite.

He'd shite in your parlour and charge you for it.

He's not only ignorant, but stingy to boot.

He'd steal the eye outta yer head and come back for the lashes.

He's a chancer and a layabout.

CÉAD MILE FÁILTE TO IRELAND

WE'LL STEAL THE EYE OUT OF YOUR HEAD & COME BACK FOR THE LASHES.

He'd wring drink out of a floozie's knickers.

He will go to any lengths to acquire alcohol (esp. for free).

JUST LAUNCHED

NEW!
WHISKEY-FLAVOURED
FLOOZIE'S KNICKERS

He got out of the wrong side of the cage this morning.

Not only is he an ignorant pig, he's also in a lousy mood.

He had a face on him as long as a donkey's back leg.

He is a dour gobshite.

He has a face like a constipated greyhound.

He is in a wojus humour.

He has a face like the divil's arse.

He is in an extremely angry and agitated state.

He has a face on him as long as a wet week in February.

He has an excessively melancholic puss on him.

He has a head on him like a bulldog licking piss off a nettle.

He is an ugly gouger.

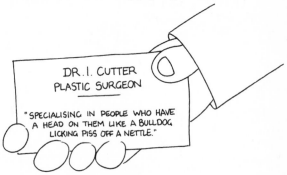

He has an arsehole at both ends of his digestive system.

He is an unpleasant bowsie who frequently talks bullshit.

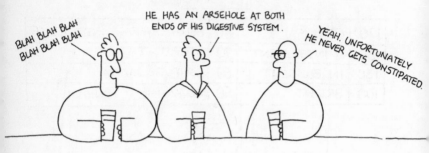

He has a photographic memory, but there's no film in the camera.

He is a complete eejit.

He has trouble spelling IQ.
He is an utter gobdaw.

	IQ RATING		
170+	GENIUS	80	BELOW AVERAGE INTELLIGENCE
150	V. INTELLIGENT	70	STUPID
130	INTELLIGENT	60	COMPLETE MORON
100	BRIGHT	50	GOVERNMENT MINISTER

He is the sap in the family tree.
In terms of intelligence, he is the black sheep
of the family.

Her arse is as wide as a Leitrim hurler's shot.
She has excessively broad buttocks.

He reminds me of the Irish sea . . .
he makes me sick.
He is a nauseating bowsie.

He was born a day late and he's been like that ever since.

He is an unreliable and unpunctual skiver.

He was premature at birth and has the same problem at conception.

He is lousy in the scratcher.

Her looks improve with distance.
She is an ugly wagon.

Her mind wandered and never came home.
She is a thick wagon.

Her weighing scale reads,
"One at a time, please."

She's a gluttonous wagon.

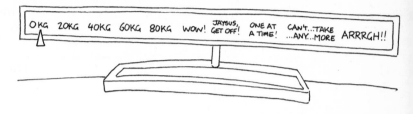

He's a few cans short of a six-pack.

He's a bit of a mentaller.

He's a few eggs short of a basket.
He's a tad nuts.

He's a few pints short of a milk churn.
He's a complete lune.

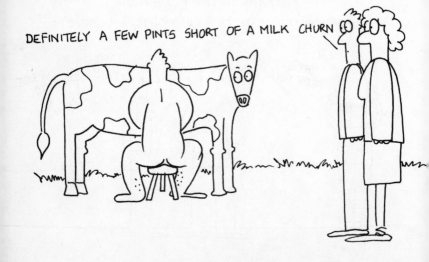

Feckin' Irish Insults

He's a neck like a jockey's bollox.
He is thick-skinned and doesn't care
what others think of him.

He sank in the gene pool.
Genetically speaking, he is a thick, ignorant sleeveen.

He's as agile as a one-armed man climbing a rope.

He is a clumsy gobshite.

> IRELAND 0   SAN MARINO 7

OUR KEEPER'S AS AGILE AS A ONE-ARMED MAN CLIMBING A ROPE.

He's as ignorant as a sack of arses.

He is a gouger completely lacking in the social graces.

YOUR HUSBAND IS AS IGNORANT AS A SACK OF ARSES.

AT LEAST AN ARSE HAS SOME FUNCTION IN LIFE.

He's as sharp as a hurley.

He's a thick gobshite.

He's like a pig knitting.

He is an awkward eejit, physically, socially, or both.

He's nobody's fool—he can't get anyone to adopt him.

He's an eejit.

He's so boring that he can't even entertain an idea.

He's a dry shite, to be avoided socially at all cost.

He's the world's first experiment in artificial stupidity.

He's a moronic gobdaw.

He supplies the entire town with natural gas.

He has uncontrollable flatulence.

He tries to be a wit but he's only halfway there.

He is excessively dense.

He wouldn't give you the steam off his piss.

He's a stingy bowsie.

He wouldn't know his langer from his thumb except for the nail.

He hasn't a clue how to interact with women,
even those of loose virtue.

HE WOULDN'T KNOW HIS LANGER FROM HIS THUMB EXCEPT FOR THE NAIL.

AND HIS THUMB'S PRETTY SMALL AT THAT.

His brain has gone home but his gob's working overtime.

He is talking bullshit.

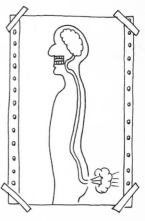

AS YOU CAN SEE FROM THIS X RAY, THE CONNECTION FROM YOUR BRAIN TO YOUR MOUTH HAS SOMEHOW GOT MIXED UP WITH THE ONE TO YOUR RECTUM. WHICH EXPLAINS WHY YOU'RE TALKING THROUGH YOUR ARSE...

His idea of helping with the housework is lifting his feet so you can vacuum.

He's a lazy, skiving dosser.

His lift doesn't go all the way to the top floor.

He's a poor thick eejit.

His mind is so open that ideas simply pass through it.

He's an absolute moron.

I bet your brain feels as good as new, seeing that you've never used it.

Mentally, you're a lazy gobdaw.

If brains were taxed, he'd be due a rebate.

He's an imbecile.

If bullshit was music, he'd be a céilí band.

He's a blatherer of the highest order.

I don't think you're a gobshite, but what's my opinion compared to thousands of others?

Everyone you know believes you to be a bowsie and a shitehawk.

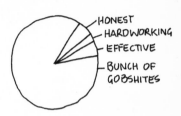

OPINION POLLS LTD.

Q: HOW WOULD YOU DESCRIBE THE CURRENT CABINET?

— HONEST
— HARDWORKING
— EFFECTIVE
— BUNCH OF GOBSHITES

If he went any slower he'd catch up with himself on the way back.

He's a painfully slow mover.

CIVIL SERVICE

JOB INTERVIEWS TODAY

MR. RICE, YOU ARRIVED 30 MINUTES LATE, IT TOOK YOU 2 HOURS TO FILL OUT THE FORM, YOU SHOW NO APTITUDE FOR ANYTHING. YOU'RE LAZY, UNAMBITIOUS AND YOU HAVE NO MANNERS. YOU'RE PERFECT FOR THE JOB.

If ignorance is bliss, she must be the happiest person alive.

She's a thick skanger.

If she ever breastfeeds, the baby will end up malnourished.

She has microscopically small boobs.

If work was a bed he'd sleep on the floor.
He is a total dosser.

I hear he was born on a farm.
There were six in the litter.
He's a manky pig.

I'm not saying he's dense, but he stared at a carton of orange juice for twenty minutes because it said "concentrate" on the label.

He's a fierce eejit.

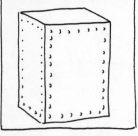

REINFORCED STEEL

DENSITY 100 MG/c³

D.4 WORKS FOR DADDY

DENSITY 500 MG/c³

I'm not saying she's thick, but when there's a wind blowing her head whistles.

She's a stupid wagon.

DUH... NOW WHERE DID I PUT MY INDEX FINGER?

Irish men are like bottles of stout—empty from the neck up.

Irish men are thoughtless gobshites.

I see your mother knows which sexual position produces the ugliest children.

You're an ugly geebag/gouger.

**It's hard to see his point of view,
as most people can't get their head
that far up their own arse.**

You're a self-obsessed sleeveen.

**It's not so much he's not playing with a full
deck, more like he's not even in the game.**

Not only is he dense, he's a bit of a lune.

I wouldn't cross Leeson Street to piss on him if his jocks were on fire.

He's a total gouger.

FIRE

IN CASE OF FIRE IN DÁIL, PLEASE BREAK TOUGHENED BULLET-PROOF, 3-INCH THICK ⟵ GLASS.

Missing a few sheep from her flock.

She's a bit of a nut case.

I'M SORRY, MRS. BO PEEP. WE DON'T DO MISSING SHEEP REPORTS.

Modesty suits him perfectly.
He has no redeeming features.

Mother Nature hates him—he reminds her of her mistakes.
He is an utter gobshite.

My car has five airbags—at least when my mother-in-law is a passenger.

My mother-in-law is an absolute wagon.

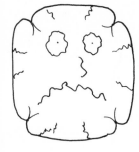

Next time you might be reincarnated as a human.

You're a complete pig.

She'd talk the teeth off a saw.
She never shuts her gob.

She fell into a pot of jam and had to eat her way out.
She's a slapper who wears too much make-up.

She has a face like a bag of spanners.
She is hideously ugly.

She has a face like the back of a turf cart.
She is physically repulsive.

She has a face on her as long as a horse's arse.
She is a sullen geebag.

She has a face on her that would turn milk.
She has an incredibly sour puss/incredibly ugly puss.

She has a face that'd stop a clock.
She is incredibly ugly.

She has a head on her like a slapped arse.
She is a brutal-looking, red-complexioned wagon.

She has an arse on her like a brewery drayhorse.

She has a colossal arse.

She's a few carrots short of a stew.

She's a bit crazy.

She's a few screams short of an orgasm.
She's a little nuts/lousy in bed.

She's a product tester for Viagra.
She's a scanger who sleeps around.

She's a walking argument for contraception.
She's a horrible geebag.

She's as exciting as a wet night in Athlone.
She's a boring wagon.

**She's bound to meet some
good-looking, successful genius.
After all, don't opposites attract?**

She is a repulsive, thick failure.

She's immune to brain damage.

She's thick.

She's not completely useless—she's a life-support system for a fanny.

She's an idiot but reputedly good in the scratcher.

WELL, DOC, IT WAS JUST ABOUT THEN THAT I TOLD HER SHE DID HAVE SOME USES— SHE WAS A LIFE SUPPORT...

She's like a bag of cats thrun into a bonfire.

She's a bad-humoured fecker.

THE WIFE'S BEEN LIKE A BAG OF CATS THRUN INTO A BONFIRE JUST 'CAUSE I DIDN'T NOTICE HER NEW DRESS.

WELL, MICK, I SUPPOSE IT WAS HER WEDDING DRESS.

She's not so much an oil painting as a mosaic.
Her complexion is brutal/she's ancient.

She's overdue for reincarnation.
She's a gobshite.

She's so boring she makes onions cry.
She's a terrible dry shite.

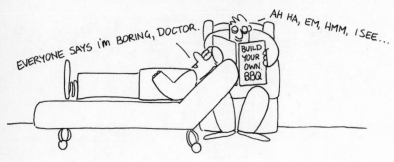

She's so fat she comes from both sides of the family tree.
She's horribly overweight.

Feckin' Irish Insults

She's so stupid she spells farm E-I-E-I-O.

She's an incredibly stupid yoke.

She's so thick she tried to put a fish out of its misery by drowning it.

She's a moron.

She's such a bad cook, she even makes a pig's dinner of feeding the pigs.

She's a lousy cook.

ACTUALLY, LOVE, I THINK YOU'LL FIND THE "BANGERS" IN "BANGERS AND MASH" USUALLY MEANS SAUSAGES.

She's the width of a Mullingar heifer.

She has a huge arse.

THEY'RE DOING LIPOSUCTION ON BIDDY MAGUIRE AGAIN.

CLINIC

She was never given the bad taste vaccine in school.

She dresses like a slapper.

That fella'd skin a fart.

He's a bowsie who'd do anything for money.

The good Lord used him for miracle practice.
He's an ugly, stupid fecker.

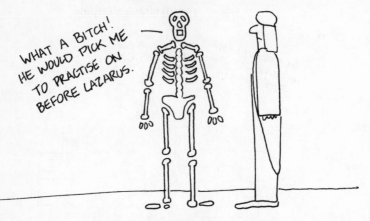

We all spring from apes, but he didn't spring far enough.
He's an uncouth gouger.

When he was born, his mother threw rocks at the stork.

He is physically repugnant.

When she walks into a room, the mice jump on chairs.

She is physically repugnant.

You big long mother's rarin'!
You are a total mammy's boy.

You smell like a slapper's handbag.
You are wearing excessive amounts of cheap perfume.

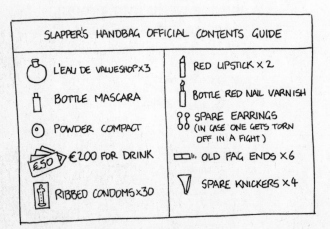

feckin'
irish
surnames

What's in a name? Well, quite a lot if you've got an Irish name. Daly, for example, which comes from the Irish word *dáil*, meaning "meeting place": today the Dáil is the official seat of the Irish Government! If you're a Lynch you gave your name to the practice of stringing people by the neck from a tree, and if you're a Kennedy your name means "helmet headed!"

The following pages bring you all the fascinating facts concerning the twenty-five most popular Irish names (along with their variants), which account for about 80 percent of all people of Irish extraction. So here's your chance to discover what a wojus shower of mucksavages you're descended from!

Byrne

Variants: *Bourne, Byrnes, O'Byrne, O'Byrnes, Burns*

Origin: The name Byrne finds its roots in Bran Mac Maolmòrrdha, the King of Leinster who kicked the bucket in the eleventh century. "Bran," luckily enough for the Byrnes, does not refer to a source of roughage but actually means "raven." Hailing originally from Kildare, the Byrne clan was forced to move to Wicklow during the Norman invasion of the twelfth century. So pissed off at having to live in Wicklow (and who can blame them?), they developed a reputation as fierce warriors in opposing the Brits. Their motto, *Certavi et Vici*, means "I have fought and conquered."

Well-known Byrnes:

- ❧ **ALFRED BYRNE** (1882–1956), was Lord Mayor of Dublin ten times

- ❧ **GABRIEL BYRNE** (b.1950), Irish actor, most recently on the TV series *In Treatment*

- ❧ **GAY BYRNE** (b.1934), legendary Irish broadcaster, host of *The Late Late Show* for thirty-seven years

- ❧ **DAVID BYRNE** (b.1952), Scottish-born musician and artist best known as founding member and songwriter of the American band Talking Heads

- ❧ **JASON BOURNE** is the fictional character in Robert Ludlum's *Bourne* novels, who is played by Matt Damon in the movie series

Connolly

Variants: *Conolly, Connally, O'Connolly, Connolley, Conally, Connelly, Conoley, Connaleigh, Connelay, Conley, Conlay, Conlaye*

Origin: Connolly derives from the old Gaelic Ó Conghaile, which itself comes from *con*, meaning "a hound," and *gal*, meaning "valour," giving us "descendant of the hound of valour." Such a shame to be descended from a dog, but hey, life's a bitch. The Ó Conghailes were originally from Connemara in the west of Ireland, a real bunch of culchies, but spread like the plague into three distinct branches in Meath, Monaghan, and in west Cork. Another religious lot, the Connollys, their motto is *En Dieu est tout*—"In God is all." One of the most famous Connollys

was William Conolly (1660–1729), who was the Speaker of the House of Commons and is said to have been the richest fecker in Ireland in his day.

OCH! YOU DINNA MEAN TAY TELL ME AFTER ALL THIS TIME I'M IRISH!*?!

Well-known Connollys:

- **BILLY CONNOLLY** (b.1942), Scottish comedian, musician, and actor, known as "The Big Yin"

- **JAMES CONNOLLY** (1868–1916), Labour leader and signatory of the Irish Declaration of Independence

- **JOHN CONNOLLY** (b.1968), Irish international bestselling author of the crime series featuring Charlie Parker, whose books include *Every Dead Thing*, *The Reapers*, and *The Lovers*

- **MICHAEL CONNELLY** (b.1956), American international best-selling crime fiction author of titles such as *The Narrows* and *The Closers*

Daly

Variants: *Daley, Daylie, Dayley, Dalley, Dailey, Daily, Dailley, Dally, O'Daily, O'Daley, O'Dalaigh*

Origins: The Daly motto is *Deo fidelis et regi*, which means "Loyal to God and king," so we know for certain that the Dalys all say their prayers and pay their taxes. Daly derives from the ancient Gaelic family name of Ó Dalaigh, which is still in use today and the word

'Dalaigh' comes from *dáil*, meaning "meeting place," and in the Daly's case the meeting place was usually the pub. The seat of the Irish government is known as Dáil Éireann, where the bullshit is so plentiful you could grow spuds in it. The chief of the O'Daly family ruled over an area that is now County Westmeath from the thirteenth century, but later started gallivanting about in neighbouring Meath and then west to Clare, where you'll still find gansey-loads of Dalys to this day.

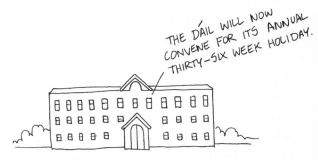

THE DÁIL WILL NOW CONVENE FOR ITS ANNUAL THIRTY-SIX WEEK HOLIDAY.

Well-known Dalys:

- **CAHAL DALY** (1917–2009), Cardinal and Primate of All Ireland
- **CEARBHALL Ó DÁLAIGH** (1911–1978), fifth President of Ireland
- **FRED DALY** (1911–1990), Irish golfer and winner of the 1947 British Open
- **TYNE DALY** (b.1946), American actress and star of television's *Cagney & Lacey*
- **JOHN DALY** (b.1946), American golfer known as "The Wild Thing," winner of the 1991 PGA Championship and the 1995 Open Championship
- **RICHARD J. DALEY** (1902–1976), Mayor of Chicago for twenty-one years

Doherty

Variants: *Docherty, Dougherty, Douherty, O'Docherty, O'Dougherty O'Douherty, and about a million others*

Origin: There are as many as 120 variations in spelling of the name Ó Dochartaigh, of which Doherty is the most common form, so they obviously aren't very good at spelling for a start. The Dohertys take their name from Dochartach, a descendant of the famous Niall of the Nine Hostages, the High King of Ireland in the fifth century, so the Doherty line stretches back donkey's years. Unfortunately *Dochartach* actually has the rather odd meaning of "hurtful" or "injurious" but the reason for this has been lost in the mists of time, i.e. cover-up. The family motto is *Ár nDuthchas*, meaning "Our heritage," but what exactly their heritage was is anyone's guess. By the fourteenth century the Ó Dochartaighs were

THE REASONS MAY BE LOST IN THE MIST OF TIME, BUT WE CAN MAKE A FEW INJURIOUS ASSUMPTIONS MR. DOHERTY...

the Lords of Inishowen, the most northerly peninsula in Ireland, but don't get too excited; in the great scheme of things Inishowen is about the size of a postage stamp.

Well-known Dohertys:

- ☙ **KEN DOHERTY** (b.1969), Irish former World Champion snooker player
- ☙ **PETER (PETE) DOHERTY** (b.1979), British rock musician
- ☙ **SHANNEN DOHERTY** (b. 1971), American actress and television director, starred in the television series *Beverly Hills 90210* and *Charmed*

Doyle

Variants: *O'Doyle, Doyill, Doill, Doile, Doyel, MacDowall*

Origin: The Gaelic name for Doyle was originally Dubhghall, which literally means "black stranger," referring to the darker hair of the Danish Viking invaders as opposed to the fair-headed Norwegians, so basically all Doyles are descended from a bunch of murdering gougers from Scandinavia. The principle counties inhabited by the Doyles (Dublin, Wexford, Wicklow, Carlow, Kerry, and Cork) are almost all coastal, reflecting the fact that they arrived by sea in search of plunder and fine holy Irish cailíns to debauch in the period 600–1000, and were then too lazy to walk any further inland. The Doyle motto is *Fortitudine Vincit*— "He conquers by fortitude"—but really means "he conquers by burying an axe in some poor eejit's head."

Well-known Doyles:

- ❧ **ARTHUR CONAN DOYLE** (1859–1930), British writer and creator of the *Sherlock Holmes* series
- ❧ **JACK DOYLE** (1913–1978), Irish boxer, Hollywood actor and singer
- ❧ **JACK DOYLE** (1869–1958), Major League Baseball player
- ❧ **RODDY DOYLE** (b.1958), Irish novelist, dramatist, and screenwriter who won the Man Booker prize in 1993, his books include *The Commitments*

Dunne

Variants: *Dunn, Dun, O'Dunne, O'Duin, O'Doyne, Doine, Doin, O'Dunn*

Origin: Dunne is derived from the old Gaelic Ó *Duinn*, meaning "dark-haired" or "dark-skinned," which probably means the Dunnes didn't wash themselves very much. The name is widespread in Ireland nowadays although the original Ó Duinn clan came from County Laois in the Irish midlands, which was once known as Queen's County after Queen "Bloody" Mary. The Dunnes were considered a threat to the English and Queen Mary robbed most of their land in the middle ages, the stupid wagon. But at one point the Dunnes were one of the most powerful

families in Leinster, and were adept at battering the bejaysus out of anyone. The Dunne motto is *Mullach Abú*, which means "Victory from the hills," so they'd basically run down from the hills, chop a few English soldiers into smithereens and then run back up again.

Well-known Dunnes:

- **BEN DUNNE** (b.1949), Irish millionaire entrepreneur and former director of Irish retail chain Dunnes Stores
- **BERNARD DUNNE** (b.1980), Irish professional boxer and former WBA Super Bantamweight World Champion
- **GRIFFIN DUNNE** (b.1955), American actor and film director whose credits include *American Werewolf in London*

Gallagher

Variants: *Galagher, Gallaher, O'Gallagher, Callacher, Callagher*

Origin: Gallagher originates from the medieval Gaelic name of Ó Gallchobhair: *gall*, meaning foreign, and *cabhair*, meaning help, i.e. a bunch of feckin' mercenaries. The Gallaghers are strongly linked to County Donegal and nowadays are chiefly found in Ulster and North Connacht, that is, if you're unlucky enough to find one. Their motto is *Mea Gloria Fides*—"Fidelity is my glory," so the Gallaghers are supposedly a trustworthy lot of mucksavages. In the fifteenth and sixteenth centuries loads of Gallaghers became well-known bishops, i.e. a bunch of bleedin' Holy Joes.

Well-known Gallaghers:

YES, SON. THE GALLAGHERS ARRIVED FROM FARAWAY LANDS BEARING ELECTRIC GUITARS

- 🐾 **LIAM GALLAGHER** (b. 1972), lead singer of the British band Oasis

- 🐾 **NOEL GALLAGHER** (b. 1967), brother of Liam, lead guitarist of Oasis

- 🐾 **PETER GALLAGHER** (b.1955), American actor whose films include *While You Were Sleeping*, also starred as Sandy Cohen in the television series *The O.C.* from 2003 to 2007

- 🐾 **RORY GALLAGHER** (1948–1995), Irish rock guitarist

Kelly

Variants: *Kelly, Kellie, O'Kelly, Kelley, Kellog, Kellyn*

Origin: Kelly originates from the Irish name Ó Ceallaigh, which came from Galway, Antrim, Meath, Sligo, and Wicklow so they talk with a whole range of culchie (Irish slang term for a rural person) accents. The name originally came from the Gaelic word *ceallach*, which means "strife" or "conflict," which means, basically, that Kellys are a lot of hassle and can be a pain in the arse. Some interpretations of their name translate as "brave warrior," so if you're ever in a battle with them, put all your Kellys in the front line. The Kelly motto is *Turris fortis mihi deus*, which means "God is a strong tower for me." One possible variant

of the name Kelly is Kellog, which is appropriate, as most Kellys are seriously flaky.

Well-known Kellys:

- **FRANK KELLY** (b.1938), Irish actor
- **GENE KELLY** (1912–1996), American actor and dancer, known for his role in the 1952 film *Singin' in the Rain*
- **GEORGE "MACHINE GUN" KELLY** (1895–1954), American gangster
- **GRACE KELLY** (1929–1982), American actress, Princess Grace of Monaco
- **LUKE KELLY** (1940–1984), Irish singer (in the band The Dubliners) and folk musician
- **NED KELLY** (c. 1854–1880), Australian outlaw

RUN FOR YOUR LIVES. THE KELLYS ARE COMING!

Kennedy

Variants: *Kenedy, Kennady, Kennead, O'Kennedy, O'Kennady, O'Kenneady*

Origin: Kennedy is of both Irish and Scottish origin and is an Anglicisation of the Gaelic *Ó Ceannéidigh*, meaning "descendant of Ceannéidigh," which, wait for it, ha ha, translates as *ceann*, meaning "head" and *éidigh*, meaning "ugly," although a slightly kinder interpretation is "helmet-headed"! These Kennedys were close allies of the powerful Dál gCais tribe of Thomond, and hailed mainly from Clare, Limerick, Mayo, and

Tipperary, but are now found in every feckin' county in Ireland, and beyond. The Kennedys have a lineage directly from Brian Boru, the great Irish chieftain, who was a son of Cennedig, head of Dal Cais, and who defeated the Vikings in 1014. The most famous Kennedy son of modern times was another great chieftain, this time of the American people. Their motto is *Avise la fin*—"Consider the end," which unfortunately poor J.F.K. clearly didn't when he decided to go to Dallas.

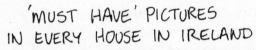

Well-known Kennedys:

- ❧ **EDWARD "TED" KENNEDY** (1932–2009), U.S. Senator
- ❧ **GEORGE KENNEDY** (b.1925), American actor noted for his roles in *Cool Hand Luke* and the *Naked Gun* film series
- ❧ **JOHN FITZGERALD KENNEDY** (1917–1963), thirty-fifth president of the United States.

Lynch

Variants: *O'Lynch, Lench, Linch, Lynch, Lynche, Linskey, Lynskey*

Origin: The original form of the name Lynch was Ó Loingsigh, a bunch of cute hoors who hailed from the west of Ireland. In fact, the Lynch family was one of the original 14 Tribes of Galway, who dominated all aspects of life in the city for over five hundred years, up to the nineteenth century (especially the pub scene). The verb "to lynch" apparently comes from a Captain William Lynch from the town of Virginia in County Cavan, who was unfortunately a keen practitioner of instant justice and would string anyone up at the drop of a hat. Alternatively, a plaque in Galway claims the word "lynch" derived from an event in 1493 when James Lynch FitzStephen, the mayor of Galway, hanged his own son from a window of his house for murdering a houseguest. The family motto is *Semper Fidelis* meaning "Always faithful," but wouldn't something like "How's it hanging?" be more appropriate?

DON'T MESS WITH THE LYNCHES

Well-known Lynchs:

- ☙ **DAVID LYNCH** (b.1946), American film director whose credits include *The Elephant Man*, *Blue Velvet*, *Mulholland Drive*, and the television series *Twin Peaks*

- ☙ **JACK LYNCH** (1917–1999), fourth Taoiseach (Prime Minister) of the Republic of Ireland

- ☙ **THOMAS LYNCH, JR.** (1749–1779), signatory of the U.S. Declaration of Independence

- ☙ **LIAM LYNCH** (1893–1923), commanding general of the Anti-Treaty Irish Republican Army during the Irish Civil War

McCarthy

Variants: *MacCarthy, MacCarty, MacArty, MacArthy, Carthy, Carty*

Origin: The McCarthy motto is *Forti et Fideli*, which means "Strong and faithful," so McCarthys never, ever have a bit on the side. Yeah, right. The name is an Anglicized version of *Mac Carthaigh*, which means "Son of the loving one," so they'd have us believe they're all nice, cuddly, and considerate types as well, just like that famous American senator from the fifties. Half of all the people with the surname in Ireland still live in County Cork, which is unfortunate for the other poor Corkonians who have to live with them. The origin of the name begins with Carthach, a king who died in 1045. His son Tadhg took his name and became the first king of Desmond, which comprised parts of Cork and Kerry and for almost five centuries they dominated much of Munster, but that's all a long time ago now, thanks be to Jaysus.

Well-known McCarthys:

- **CORMAC McCARTHY** (b. 1933), American novelist whose books include *The Road* and *No Country For Old Men*
- **JOSEPH RAYMOND McCARTHY** (1908–1957), US Senator whose extreme anti-communist actions were coined "McCarthyism" in the 1950s
- **KEVIN McCARTHY** (1914–2010), American actor whose credits include roles in *Death of a Salesman* and *Invasion of the Body Snatchers*
- **MARY McCARTHY** (1912–1989), American author of *The Group* (1963), which remained on the *New York Times* Best Seller List for almost two years
- **MICK McCARTHY** (b. 1959), Irish football player and former manager of Republic of Ireland

McLaughlin

Variants: *MacLaughlin, O'Loughlin, Loughnane, McLaglen*

Origin: The McLaughlin motto is *Anchora salutis*, which means "A face like a cow's back-side." No, only kidding, it really means, "The anchor of salvation." The name McLaughlin comes from two distinct gangs of bogtrotters. One strand of ancestry has a royal connection—that of Ó Maoilsheachlainn, a descendant of Malachy II, High King of Ireland from 980 to 1002, when he had his arse kicked and was dethroned by Brian Boru. The other strand comes from the Mac Lochlainn family of Donegal and Derry, who were a branch of the ruling Uí Neill clan, and some say were the sap in the family tree.

Well-known McLaughlins:

- **ROBERT E. McLAUGHLIN** (1908–1973), *TIME* magazine editor, author, and playwright
- **GEORGE VINCENT McLAUGHLIN** (1887–1967), President of the Brooklyn Trust Company and New York City Police Commissioner from 1926–1927
- **VICTOR McLAGLEN** (1886–1959), Academy Award-winning English actor who starred opposite John Wayne in *The Quiet Man*

Moore

Variants: *More, Moor, O'More, Moores, Mores, McMore, Moire, Moare, MacMoore, McMoir, Moir, Moors, O'Moore, O'Moire, McMoare, MacMoir, MacMoare, Mooer*

Origin: The name Moore, although closely linked to Ireland, has several distant origins, i.e. they're from all over the gaff. The Irish tie is from the ancient Irish clan of Ó Mordha, from the Gaelic word *mordha*, meaning "stately" or "noble," who were a powerful gang of feckers in parts of Leinster and Munster. There is also a yonks-old Gaelic-Manx link to the Isle of Mann named Moar. Yet another connection to the Moore name is that of the Moor, which implies North African descent, so they certainly sowed their wild oats far and wide. However the Moores' strongest connections are to Ireland and the name and its many variants are found in every arse-end of nowhere throughout the country. The Moore motto is the strange *Conlan Abú*, which means "Conlan forever," Conlan probably referring to a fifteenth century head-the-ball and chieftain.

Well-known Moores:

- **HENRY MOORE** (1898–1986), British artist and sculptor
- **THOMAS MOORE** (1779–1852), renowned Irish poet and songwriter of Moore's Melodies, including *The Last Rose of Summer*, *The Minstrel Boy*, and many more
- **JULIANNE MOORE** (b.1960), American actress whose films include *The Big Lebowski*, *The End of the Affair*, and *The Hours*
- **MARY TYLER MOORE** (b.1936), American actress and comedian, star of television's *The Mary Tyler Moore Show*
- **MICHAEL MOORE** (b.1954), American documentary filmmaker whose credits include *Bowling for Columbine* and *Fahrenheit 9/11*
- **ROGER MOORE** (b.1927), British actor best known for playing James Bond in seven movies, from 1973 to 1985

Murphy

Variants: *Morphy, O'Murphy, MacMurphy, Morfey*

Origin: Murphy is the most popular surname in Ireland. Everywhere you go you'll find Murphys by the ganseyload; they're all over the place. Which naturally leads to the inevitable conclusion that male Murphys, as a rule, are incredibly virile and much sought after by women. The name derives from the old Irish names Ó Murchadha (descendant of Murchadh), and Mac Murchaidh (son of Murchadh), and roughly translated means "sea warrior." According to the *Oxford English Dictionary*, Murphy derives from the Greek God of Dreams, Morpheus, but that's probably a load of crap. Originally the Murphy clan hailed from Wexford, Armagh, Tyrone, Carlow, and especially Cork, where they are still breeding like rabbits. The Murphy motto is *Fortis et hospitalis*, which means "Brave and hospitable," so they're probably good to drop in on if you're looking for a few free drinks. It's pretty certain that whatever first name you were given by your parents, as a Murphy your nickname will be "Spud."

HELLO, MRS MURPHY.
I HEARD YOU WERE OUT
WITH THE MURPHYS
IN MURPHY'S LAST
NIGHT.

Well-known Murphys:

- **AUDIE MURPHY** (1925–1971), American war hero and actor
- **CILLIAN MURPHY** (b.1976), Irish actor whose credits include roles in the movies *Batman Begins* and *The Dark Knight*
- **EDDIE MURPHY** (b.1961), American actor and comedian who gained fame on TV's *Saturday Night Live* and the *Beverly Hills Cop* film series
- **COLIN MURPHY** (b.1959), Incredibly talented and good-looking author of the *Feckin'* book series
- **ALEX JAMES MURPHY** was the name of the police officer who became Robocop in the 1987 movie *Robocop*
- **R.P. McMURPHY** was the main character in the book *One Flew Over the Cuckoo's Nest*; the role was played by Jack Nicholson in the 1975 movie of the same name

Murray

Variants: *O'Murray, MacMurray, Murray, MacMorrow, Gilmore*

Origin: Although extremely popular in Ireland, the name Murray (which means "by the sea") probably originated from a shower of mucksavages in the Moray region of Scotland. Every day they would have a gander at Ulster across the Irish Sea and eventually decided to leg it out of Scotland and come over and chat up our fine Northern Irish lassies, and who could blame them? In fact they got on so well that they multiplied like rabbits and to this day the Murrays are all over Ulster like zits

on a teen's face. The Murray motto is *Tout prêt*, meaning "Always prepared," so they also fancy themselves as a bunch of boy scouts. There is also a branch of Murrays who derive from the old Irish family of Ó Muireadhaigh who hailed from County Roscommon, but the less said about those sleeveens, the better.

Well-known Murrays:

- **ANDY MURRAY** (b.1987), the top-ranked British tennis player
- **BILL MURRAY** (b.1950), American movie actor whose credits include *Ghostbusters*, *Groundhog Day*, and *Lost in Translation*
- **MURRAY HAMILTON** (1923–1986), American movie actor who played the mayor in *Jaws*

O'Brien

Variants: *O'Bryan, O'Brian, O'Breen, Breen, Bryant*

Origin: The O'Briens can trace a proud lineage all the way back to the great Brian Boru, who battered the living crap out of the Vikings at Clontarf in 1014. Their name now established, the sept (clan) took a shine to many a Munster *cailín*, each of whom produced a hurling team of new little O'Briens, becoming so populous that they soon were bedded down (literally) as the dominant sept in Limerick, Tipperary, Clare, and Waterford.

In fact it's still hard to give someone a clatter in these areas without hitting an O'Brien. Their motto, *Lámh láidir in uachtar*, roughly means "The strongest arm rules," or some such oul' guff. The O'Briens are reputedly one of the five septs who are cursed with being able to hear the banshee's wail, which foretells a death in the family, so at least they're good for something.

Well-known O'Briens:

- **AIDAN O'BRIEN** (b.1969), Irish race horse trainer whose wins include the Prix de l'Arc de Triomphe, the Ascot Gold Cup, and the Breeders Cup Marathon
- **VINCENT O'BRIEN** (1917–2009), Irish race horse trainer who was the winner of some of the world's most prestigious races, his horses included the great Nijinsky
- **CONAN O'BRIEN** (b.1963), American talk show host and comedian
- **EDNA O'BRIEN** (b.1930), award-winning Irish novelist
- **FLANN O'BRIEN** (1911–1966), *nom de plume* of Irish novelist Brian O'Nolan who is best known for *At-Swim-Two Birds* and *The Third Policeman*
- **MARGARET O'BRIEN** (b.1937), American child actress who appeared in more than twenty films, from *Babes on Broadway* with Mickey Rooney to *Meet Me In St. Louis* with Judy Garland

O'Carroll

Variants: *O'Carrol, Carroll, Carrel, Carrell, Carrill, Carrol, Caroll, Caryll, Garvil, Garvill*

Origin: The O'Carroll motto is *In fide et in bello fortes*, meaning "Strong in faith and war," so basically they were a bunch of holy Joes and savages. In old texts, this ancient name appears as both MacCarroll and O'Carroll. Its origins are from the old Gaelic names of Mac Cearbhaill or Ó Cearbhaill, from the word *cearbh*, meaning "to hack" or "to chop," which probably refers to the use of a weapon by a warrior to cut lumps out of some poor gobshite. There were two clans of MacCarroll (mostly in Ulster) and six of O'Carroll (mostly in Leinster), and nowadays Kerry, Offaly, Monaghan, Tipperary, Leitrim, Meath, and Louth are all crawling with O'Carroll feckers.

MRS. CARROLL. MY JOHNNY DOESN'T WANT TO PLAY WITH YOUR SON ANYMORE...

Well-known O'Carrolls:

- **LEWIS CARROLL**, pseudonym of British author Charles Lutwidge Dodgson (1832–1898), author of *Alice's Adventures in Wonderland*

- **DIAHANN CARROLL** (b.1935), American award-winning actress and singer

- **STEVE CARELL** (b.1962), American actor, Golden Globe winner for his role on the television series *The Office*

O'Connell

Variants: *Connell, O'Connell, Cannell, Connall, Conell, Conall, Connill, Connull, Connel, Connal, Connul, Canell, Cannel, O'Connall, O'Conell*

Origin: O'Connell is a famous surname whose origins stretch back further than a floozie's knicker elastic. It literally means "descendant of Congall," which, like Connolly, comes from *con,* "a hound" or "wolf," and *gal,* meaning "valour" or "strength," i.e. a pack of feckin' wild animals. In fact, the O'Connell clan claims descent that goes all the way back to Aengus Tuirmeach, who was High King of Ireland around 200 BC, although this could be a load of old blather. The family motto is *Ciall agus neart,*

meaning "Reason and power," which at least is in Irish and not ganky Latin or French. The O'Connells are most populous nowadays in County Kerry in the southwest of Ireland, which is the birthplace of the most famous of the clan—Daniel O'Connell, The Liberator, who did his very best to boot the Brits out of Ireland. Fair play to ye, Daniel!

Well-known O'Connells:

- **DANIEL O'CONNELL** (1775–1847), known as "The Liberator," one of Ireland's greatest statesman, responsible for Catholic Emancipation
- **JERRY O'CONNELL** (b.1974), American actor whose credits include *Sliders*, *Stand By Me*, and television's *Crossing Jordan*
- **MICK O'CONNELL** (b.1937), legendary Kerry Gaelic football player and coach
- **PAUL O'CONNELL** (b.1979), Irish international rugby player and team captain

O'Connor

Variants: *Connor, Conner, Conor, Connors, O'Connor, Connores, Conner, Connar, Connars, O'Connar, O'Conner, Connair, etc., etc., etc.*

Origin: If you're an O'Connor you're in luck as God is on your side, at least according to your family motto, which is *From God every help.* Your name goes back a long way—about a thousand years in fact, to the King of Connacht, Conchobhar, who died about 970 and whose name translates to "lover of hounds." Apparently he was a lover of the girls as well, as he sired so many children that the O'Connors spread out to virtually every corner of Ireland and beyond. To underline the point, there are nearly as many variations on the O'Connor name as there are actual O'Connors and the list of celebrities who bear the name is as long as *War And Peace.*

Well-known O'Connors:

- **C.Y. O'CONNOR** (1843–1902), Legendary Irish-Australian civil engineer
- **CHRISTY O'CONNOR, SR.** (b. 1924), Irish golfer with ten appearances on Ryder Cup Team, elected to World Golf Hall of Fame 2009
- **FRANK O'CONNOR** (1903–1966), Irish author
- **SINÉAD O'CONNOR** (b. 1966), Irish singer-songwriter
- **JOSEPH O'CONNOR** (b. 1963), Irish novelist, author of *Star of the Sea*
- **CARROLL O'CONNOR** (1924–2001), American actor, producer, and director who starred as Archie Bunker in the '70s TV series *All in the Family*
- **JOHN JOSEPH O'CONNOR** (1920–2000), Cardinal, Archbishop of New York from 1984–2000

O'Neill

Variants: *O'Neil, O'Neall, O'Neal*

Origin: The name O'Neill is closely associated with Ulster so if you'd like to practice their original accent try this: instead of saying "How now brown cow," say "Hoiw noiw brian coiw."

Got that? No? Never mind. The symbol of Ulster, the Red Hand, was actually nicked from the O'Neill coat of arms and their motto is *Lámh Dearg Érin Abú*, meaning "The red hand of Ireland forever." County Tyrone was the family seat since antiquity, not to mention the family bed, family table, family desk, and family closet. O'Neill means "offspring of Niall," probably referring to the once High King of Ireland, Niall of the Nine Hostages, who died around 450.

HM... WHAT SYMBOL WILL I USE FOR MY COAT OF ARMS?

Well-known O'Neills:

- **EUGENE O'NEILL** (1888–1953), American dramatist, Nobel prizewinner, author of *Long Day's Journey Into Night*

- **TIP O'NEILL** (1912–1994), former Speaker of the U.S. House of Representatives

- **RYAN O'NEAL** (b. 1941), American actor
- **TATUM O'NEAL** (b. 1963), American actress, daughter of Ryan O'Neal

O'Reilly

Variants: *O'Reilley, O'Reily, O'Rielly, O'Riely, O'Riley, O'Rilley, Reel*

Origin: O'Reilly comes from the Gaelic Ó *Raghallaigh* which, loosely translated, means "outgoing people," outgoing to the nearest bar usually. Nowadays the name is common throughout Ireland, but especially in County Cavan, where people are reputedly so mean they'd steal the eye out of your head and come back for the lashes.

O'Reillys are also common to a lesser degree in Longford, Meath, Westmeath, and Monaghan. In fact they're generally as common as muck. The O'Reillys had a reputation as expert

THOSE O'REILLYS ARE CLEVER FINANCIERS!

financiers and in the fifteenth century they even created their own coinage, most of which remains sewn into their pockets to this day. Their motto is *Fortitudine et Prudential*, meaning "By fortitude and prudence," i.e. I'm a mean gobshite.

Well-known O'Reillys:

- **JOHN C. REILLY** (b.1965), Irish-American actor who appeared in the movies *Chicago*, *Gangs of New York*, *The Hours*, and more
- **ALEJANDRO O'REILLY** (1722–1794), Irish-Spanish general and Spanish governor of Louisiana
- **SIDNEY REILLY** (1874–1925), infamous spy who was thought to have worked for at least four nations, used by Ian Fleming as model for the character James Bond
- **TONY O'REILLY** (b.1936), Irish billionaire businessman, former CEO of Heinz, dominant shareholder of Independent News and Media, and Waterford Wedgwood

O'Sullivan

Variants: *Sullivan, Sullavan*

Origin: There are two interpretations of the origin of the O'Sullivan name. One is that it comes from the Irish name Ó Súilleabháin, which translates as "grandson of the one-eyed," and the other from the older Irish version Ó Súildhubhán, which means "grandson of the dark-eyed." There is no truth in the rumour that it can also translate as "grandson of the gee-eyed," though to look at most O'Sullivans, you might wonder. They first made their appearance in Tipperary, but then

began popping up in Cork and Kerry in alarming numbers, and this is where you're still most likely to find one, if for some strange reason you wanted to go and look for one. Their motto is *An Lámh Fhoisteanach Abú*, which means "The steady hand to victory," but considering how much O'Sullivans drink, steady hands are a rarity among them.

Well-known O'Sullivans:

- ❧ **GILBERT O'SULLIVAN** (b.1946), Irish singer-songwriter who had many international hits in the '70s

- ❧ **MAUREEN O'SULLIVAN** (1911–1998), Irish-American actress who played "Jane" to Johnny Weissmuller's "Tarzan," mother of actress Mia Farrow

- ❧ **RONNIE O'SULLIVAN** (b.1975), three times world champion English snooker player

- ❧ **SONIA O'SULLIVAN** (b.1969), Irish World Champion runner and Olympic medalist

- ❧ **THE SULLIVAN BROTHERS,** five American siblings who died after their ship was sunk in WWII. The U.S. Navy named two destroyers *The Sullivans* to honor the brothers, and laws were passed to separate siblings in combat. A film, *The Fighting Sullivans*, tells their story.

Quinn

Variants: *O'Quinn, Quin, Quinn, Quine, MacQuin, MacQuinn, McQuin, McQuinn, MacCuin, Cuinn, Cuin*

Origin: The Quinn motto is *Quae Sursum Volo Videri*, meaning "I would see what is above."

What in the name of Jaysus that means is anyone's guess, but it could refer to the Quinn's legendary love of getting langered, i.e. extremely drunk, then falling down and spending the night looking at the heavens, but who knows? Quinn has been the most popular name in County Tyrone for donkey's years. It is derived from the old Irish name Ó Cuinn, meaning descendants of Conn, which means "wisdom" or "chief," so Quinns are supposed to be a bright bunch of bowsies. Outside of Tyrone, an ancient Gaelic Quinn family gave the village of Inchiquin in Clare its name, where Quinn descendants continue to get rat-arsed to this day.

WE WOULD ALL "SEE WHAT IS ABOVE" IF NIALL QUINN WASN'T STANDING IN FRONT OF US.

Well-known Quinns:

- **AIDAN QUINN** (b.1959), Irish-American actor whose credits include *Desperately Seeking Susan*, *Legends of the Fall*, and *Michael Collins*

- **ANTHONY QUINN** (1915–2001), Irish-Mexican-American actor whose films include *Zorba the Greek*, *Lawrence of Arabia*, and *The Guns of Navarone*
- **TERRY O'QUINN** (b.1952), American actor most famous for playing the character of Locke on the television series *Lost*

Ryan

Variants: *O'Ryan, Mulrian, Mulryan, O'Mulrian*

Origin: Ryan is a derivative of the old Gaelic word *righ*, which means "king," but don't get yourself carried away now with notions of a royal bloodline, particularly as there are so many Ryans you can't all be feckin' kings and queens. In actual fact, Ryan literally means "little king," which means your ancestors probably had dominion over an area about the size of a postage stamp. The Ryan motto is *Malo More Quam Foedari*, which means "I would rather die than be disgraced," something to remember the next time you're staggering rat-arsed out of the pub having puked on the barmaid's dress. The Ryans originally hailed from Tipperary and Limerick.

I MAY BE SMALL BUT I'M PERFECTLY FORMED

Well-known Ryans:

- **CORNELIUS RYAN** (1920–1974) Irish-American journalist and author of *A Bridge too Far*
- **ROBERT RYAN** (1909–1973), Hollywood actor
- **MEG RYAN** (b.1961), American actress, who has starred in such blockbuster movies as *When Harry Met Sally* and *Sleepless in Seattle*

Walsh

Variants: *Walch, Walshe, Welch, Welsh, Wellch, Wellsh, Wollch, Wallsh, Branagh, Brannagh*

Origin: When Strongbow launched his invasion of Ireland in 1171, he brought with him a horde of ugly, foul-smelling muck-savages. These were the original Walshes. At the time they were called *Breathnach*, which basically means Brits, or in the case of Strongbow's particular army, Welshmen. Thus we get Walsh directly from Welsh. The Walshes spread out and eventually found the *cailíns* of Mayo and Kilkenny most to their liking, producing countless more little Walshes, who are still found mostly in these counties today. Their motto is the appropriately bizarre *Transfixus sed non mortuus*, which means "Pierced but not dead."

Well-known Walshes:

- **JOE WALSH** (b.1947), American guitarist and rock musician with the Eagles
- **J.T. WALSH** (1943–1998), American movie actor, played Sgt. Major Dickerson in the 1987 movie *Good Morning Vietnam*

- **M. EMMET WALSH** (b.1935), American movie actor whose most notable role was as Bryant in Ridley Scott's cult classic *Blade Runner*
- **LOUIS WALSH** (b.1952), Irish pop music manager whose roster included Boyzone and Westlife

feckin'
irish
trivia

Here's an interesting piece of trivia: "trivia" comes from the Latin words *tri* and *via*, meaning three roads. This was where people met and exchanged useless chit-chat. And this was never more true than for Irish folk, who especially like to meet in pubs and swap loads of fascinating bits of oul' blather.

Did you know, for example, that although nudism is illegal in Ireland, a recent survey listed Hawk Cliff, Dublin and Inch Beach, Kerry as two of the top ten best beaches in the world to let it all hang out?!? Or that Irish physicist John Tyndall was the first man to explain why the sky is blue? Or that Montgomery Street in Dublin was once the largest red light district in all of Europe! A whole world of useless Irish blather awaits . . .

Muckanaghederdauhaulia (22 letters), in Co. Galway is the **LONGEST PLACENAME** in Ireland. It is a townland and port and is the longest port name in the world.

Although **NUDISM** is illegal in Ireland, a recent survey listed Hawk Cliff, Dalkey, Co. Dublin and Inch Beach, Dingle, Co. Kerry as two of the top ten best beaches in the world to let it all hang out.

Two of Britain's most **INFAMOUS MURDERERS**, Burke and Hare, who used to smother the elderly residents of their lodging house in Edinburgh and sell the bodies for medical research, were Irish. When Burke was hanged, his body was donated to the medical school. A pocketbook made of his skin is on display at the Police Museum on the Royal Mile in Edinburgh.

Forty million Americans claim Irish lineage.

An ancient Irish marriage ritual called "handfasting" involved tying a rope between the newlyweds' wrists for 366 days. It is said that this is where the expression **"TYING THE KNOT"** originated.

Montgomery Street in Dublin was once the largest **RED LIGHT DISTRICT** in all of Europe, with over 1,600 prostitutes plying their trade. A song called "Take Me Up To Monto" sung by the Dubliners memorializes this area.

The **SMALLEST** ever Irishman was David Jones from Lisburn in Co. Antrim, who stood at 2 feet 2 inches when he died in 1970, aged 67.

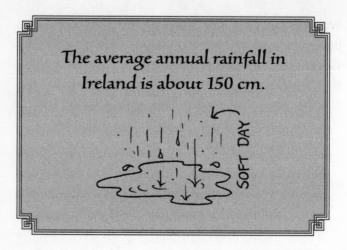

The average annual rainfall in Ireland is about 150 cm.

SOFT DAY

The Irish band **THIN LIZZY** took their name from a *Dandy* comic book robot character called "Tin Lizzie."

There are twelve towns or cities in the US called Dublin.

Montserrat, an island in the Caribbean, is the only other state that celebrates **ST. PATRICK'S DAY**, as most of its population's ancestors were Irish slaves sent there by the English.

WILLIAM HILL, one of Britain's biggest and well-known bookmakers, was a Black and Tan in Ireland in 1919, stationed in Mallow, Co. Cork.

The original Irish Houses of Parliament (which sat in what is now the Bank of Ireland, College Green, Dublin), was the **WORLD'S FIRST** purpose-built two-chamber parliament house.

In 1952, one member of the **CENSORSHIP BOARD** reviewed seventy books in a three-month period and banned all seventy.

Ireland's St. Fiacre, born in the sixth century, is the patron saint of gardeners.

DEAR ST. FIACRE. PLEASE ERADICATE THESE POXY SLUGS IN MY GARDEN. AMEN.

Ballygally Castle in Co. Antrim, nowadays a hotel, is said to be one of the **MOST HAUNTED** places in Ireland, thanks to Lady Isobel Shaw, who supposedly knocks on doors at night. Lady Isobel was reputedly locked in her room and starved by her husband during the seventeenth century, until she finally leapt to her death from a window.

NIGHT NIGHT.
— SWEET DREAMS!

Many historians believe that the game of rugby was invented, not as is commonly believed, when William Webb Ellis picked up the ball and ran at **RUGBY** School in England, but that his father, an officer, had been based in Ireland where he witnessed the game of *Caid* being played—which involved much physical contact, running with a ball, and trying to get it across a boundary, and that his son was simply demonstrating this sport. So the Irish, not the English, invented rugby!

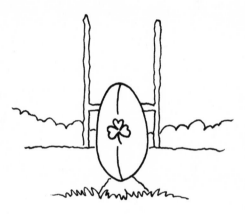

Hitler's sister-in-law was an Irish woman called Bridget Dowling.

The cliffs at Croaghaun, Achill Island, at 668 m, are said to be the **HIGHEST SEA CLIFFS** in Europe.

Clare is known as "The Banner County" because of its former tradition of carrying banners to political meetings.

The '70s Celtic Rock Band **HORSLIPS** took their name from a spoonerism on "The Four Horsemen of the Apocalypse," which became "The Four Poxmen on The Horslypse," eventually shortened to "Horslips."

Ireland's most **FAMOUS WITCH** was Dame Alice Kyteler, born in Co. Kilkenny in 1280. All four of her husbands died, and she was accused of poisoning them. In 1325, on the night before she was to be burned at the stake, she escaped and is believed to have fled to England. Her maid and follower, Petronilla de Meath, was burned instead. She was the first person in Ireland to be burned at the stake for witchcraft.

The geographical centre of Ireland is at a point in **ROSCOMMON**, 3 km south of Athlone.

The Irish alphabet does not contain the letters J, K, Q, V, W, X, Y, or Z.

The infamous Nazi propaganda broadcaster, William Joyce, aka **LORD HAW HAW**, was raised and educated in Galway.

The Europa Hotel in Belfast is the world's most **BOMBED HOTEL**, having been blasted thirty-three times.

The real name of Dublin's Ha'penny Bridge is the Liffey Bridge.

Foxrock, Co. Dublin, is said to be the only village in Ireland **WITHOUT A PUB**.

St. Brendan is said to have discovered America a thousand years before Columbus.

COOOL! IS THIS PLACE LIKE, AWESOME OR WHAT?

In 1944 the **CATHOLIC HIERARCHY** asked the Minister for Public Health to ban tampons as they might "stimulate young girls at an impressionable age," and the Government happily complied.

More than 150,000 Irish men fought in the American Civil War.

Irish physicist John Tyndall (1820–1893) was the first person to explain why the **SKY IS BLUE**.

SEE, IT'S STOPPED
RAINING. THAT'S WHY
THE SKY IS BLUE.

The lowest ever **AIR TEMPERATURE** recorded in Ireland was –19.1°C at Markree Castle, Co. Sligo on January 16, 1881.

MARKREE CASTLE

The phrase **"BY HOOK OR BY CROOK"** is said to have been coined by Richard de Clare, aka Strongbow, during the Norman invasion of Ireland when he stated that he would take Waterford by landing his army at either Hook Head or by Crook village.

Between the 1930s and 1950s, the government employed hundreds of people to physically cut **LINGERIE ADS** out of foreign magazines, as they were considered to be of a sexually arousing nature.

According to Teagasc, the Irish Agriculture and Food Development Authority, almost 10 percent of Ireland's entire **BARLEY CROP** is used in the making of Guinness beer.

Irish-American architect Louis Henri Sullivan is credited with the invention of the skyscraper.

During the Easter 1916 Rising, food for the big cats in **DUBLIN ZOO** was in such short supply that they killed some of the other animals to feed them.

In the 1934 Ireland v. Belgium World Cup qualifier, which ended 4–4, Paddy Moore of the **SHAMROCK ROVERS** became the first player in the world to score four goals in a World Cup game.

KEEP ON HOOPIN' PADDY.

Up to the late 1960s, women who had given birth were supposed to attend a ceremony called **"CHURCHING,"** which involved them being blessed and "made pure again."

261 people in Ireland have had a heart transplant.

The largest **METEORITE** ever recorded in Ireland or Britain was part of a shower that fell in Limerick on September 10, 1813. It weighed 48 kg.

Astronomer Agnes Mary Clerke (1842–1907) from Skibbereen is the only Irish person to have a **LUNAR CRATER** named after her.

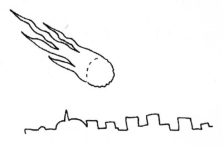

The word **"STEEPLECHASE"** originated in 1752 from a cross-country horse race between the steeples of Buttevant Church to St. Leger Church in Doneraile, Co. Cork.

Dublin's last workhouse, in Smithfield, only closed down in 1969.

Before the ban on **CONTRACEPTION** was lifted in Ireland in the mid-1980s, it was fairly common practice to use clingfilm as a substitute for condoms.

When the army blew up the remaining stump of
NELSON'S PILLAR in 1966, they shattered hundreds
of windows in O'Connell Street, Dublin, causing far more
damage than when Republicans toppled the 40-metre-high
column with a bomb two days earlier.

*Up to 1892 there were twenty-one
players on a GAA team,
six more than at present.*

While filming **RYAN'S DAUGHTER** in 1970–71, David Lean famously waited for one year so he could shoot in a storm of sufficient ferocity.

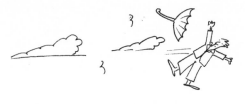

IS THIS WINDY ENOUGH MR. LEEEEAN?

Patrick Cotter O'Brien (1760–1806), from Kinsale, was the **TALLEST** Irishman ever—8 feet 1 inch—and one of only twelve people in medical history to measure over eight feet.

The two species of **RAT** in Ireland are the black and the brown, but the black rat is exclusive to the tiny Lambay Island off the coast of Dublin.

— HEY! WHAT ABOUT OUR NEAR RELATIVES UP IN LEINSTER HOUSE?

THOMAS BRACKEN from Monaghan, who became a successful poet in New Zealand in the late nineteenth century, wrote New Zealand's National Anthem.

In ancient Celtic Ireland you could divorce your partner because he/she was too fat.

During an episode of the **LATE LATE SHOW** in the sixties, Gay Byrne held a mock version of "Mr. & Mrs.," during which he asked a contestant what she wore on her honeymoon night. When she replied "nothing" there was a torrent of complaints and condemnation.

The **BIGGEST ROBBERY** in the history of the Irish Republic was on February 26, 2009, when 7 million euro were stolen from the Bank of Ireland on College Green, Dublin.

In 1916 rebels seized the Dublin Wireless School of Telegraphy and began sending a message in Morse code, continuing for several days: "Irish Republic declared in Dublin today. Irish troops have captured city and are in full possession. Enemy cannot move in city. The whole country rising." This is generally accepted as the **WORLD'S FIRST RADIO BROADCAST**.

During the first half of the nineteenth century, the average number of **CHILDREN** per household in Ireland was ten.

Girlie magazines like *Playboy* were banned in Ireland until 1996.

In 1991, Irishman **DANIEL O'DONNELL** occupied six of the top seven places in the UK Country Music charts.

Ireland is the only country in the world to have a musical instrument, **THE HARP**, as its national symbol.

In 2002 a couple was arrested by the Gardaí, having been caught having sex in the centre of **CROKE PARK** in the middle of the night.

I'VE ALWAYS WANTED TO SCORE IN CROKER.

The word **"DONNYBROOK,"** meaning a large fracas, originated from Donnybrook Fair, the annual scene of much drunken brawling, so much, in fact, that the fair was banned in 1855.

The **CAPSTONE** of the Brownshill Dolmen in County Carlow weighs approximately 100 metric tons and is the heaviest such megalithic stone in Europe.

There are four cows for every person in County Laois.

The first floodlit GAA game in Croke Park in 2007 between Dublin and Tyrone was disrupted by Croke Park's first ever **STREAKER**, a nineteen-year-old man.

Muhammad Ali's great grandfather was Irish. Abe Grady was born in Ennis in 1842.

The fight between John Wayne and Victor McLaglen in *The Quiet Man* is the **LONGEST BRAWL** in cinema history.

In pre-Christian Ireland **POLYGAMY** was widely practised.

The remains of **ST. VALENTINE**, the patron saint of love, whose feast day is celebrated on February 14, are buried in Dublin's Whitefriar Street church.

BUCK WHALEY was the notorious gambling, hard-drinking, whoring son of a wealthy landowner in the late eighteenth century, who, at the age of sixteen, lost £14,000 in a single night in a Paris casino (millions in today's money). He would accept virtually any bet, and when challenged to live on Irish soil while residing outside the country, he duly imported tons of Irish soil to the Isle of Man and built a house on it.

Hurling is the world's fastest field team sport.

German pilots believed they were over a British city when they **DROPPED BOMBS** on Dublin in 1941. Thirty-eight people died.

Nuns used to ban girls from wearing **SHINY SHOES** in the fifties and sixties in case boys could see the girls' knickers in the reflection.

At one point, pre-Gaelic Athletic Association, sliotars (hurling balls) were made of hollow bronze.

VIAGRA, the famous drug that's been giving people's sex lives a lift the world over, was mass-produced for the first time in Ringaskiddy, Co. Cork.

The world-famous **BOOK OF KELLS** was made from the skin of about two hundred cows and the ink from a mixture of apple juice and soot.

In 1845, William Parsons built a 183 cm **REFLECTING TELESCOPE** near Birr in Co. Offaly, which remained the largest telescope in the world for seventy years.

Up to the thirteenth century in Ireland it was commonplace for **PRIESTS** and **MONKS** to have wives, girlfriends, and children.

FATHER, CAN I HAVE MY POCKETMONEY?

Fungi the Dolphin has been resident in Dingle Bay for over a quarter of a century.

Jackie Carey of Manchester United captained Ireland when they beat England 2–0 in Goodison Park in 1949, becoming the first team to **DEFEAT ENGLAND AT HOME**. Carey played in nine different positions in his career, including goalkeeper.

The **TALLEST STRUCTURE** in the Republic of Ireland is the transmitter near Tullamore, Co. Offaly, which stands at 290 m.

Dublin's O'Connell Bridge is wider than it is long.

Two hundred and fifty million years ago, Ireland was at the same **LATITUDE** as present day Egypt.

IT'S A TAD WARM   MUSTN'T COMPLAIN.

The name of the British political party, the **TORIES**, originates from an old Gaelic word *toraidhe*, meaning "plunderer."

LOUGH REE, situated on the Shannon, between Longford and Westmeath, is said to be home to a Loch Ness–type monster.

JAYSUS IT'S AMAZING THE STUFF YOU SEE AFTER DRINKING A BOTTLE OF TURPENTINE

In 1940–41 **HITLER'S** propaganda minister, Joseph Goebbels, commissioned two anti-British, pro-Irish rebel movies called *The Fox of Glenarvon* and *My Life for Ireland*, with German actors playing all the Irish roles.

Dublin has 1147.3 people per square km.

The highest ever **ATTENDANCE** at a sporting event in Ireland was 90,556, at the 1961 All-Ireland Senior Football Final between Offaly and Down.

Well-known Irish movie actor **COLIN FARRELL** auditioned to become a member of the successful boyband Boyzone, but was rejected.

The sun sets in Galway almost one full hour after it has set in London.

VALENTIA ISLAND in Co. Kerry is the most westerly point in Europe that is inhabited.

Because **HENRY MOORE**, Earl of Drogheda, owned land in Dublin, he decided to name a street or two after himself as the land was developed. Thus we got Henry Street, Moore Street, North Earl Street, and Drogheda Street, which is now O'Connell Street.

The **SMALLEST IRISHWOMAN** on record was Catherine Kelly who died in England in 1785 and was just 2 feet 10 inches tall.

The Titanic, which was built in Ireland, cost $7.5 million to build. The movie Titanic cost $200 million.

A survey on www.tripadvisor.com voted the **BLARNEY STONE** the most unhygienic tourist attraction in the world.

On www.tripadvisor.com the same survey voted **OSCAR WILDE'S TOMB** in Père Lachaise Cemetery, Paris, as the third most unhygienic tourist attraction—it is covered in lipstick prints!

MAUMTRASNA MOUNTAIN on the Galway-Mayo border covers a total surface area of almost 40 square km.

When **RED HUGH O'DONNELL** escaped from Dublin Castle in 1592, along with Art and Henry O'Neill, they became the only prisoners ever to successfully escape captivity in Dublin Castle.

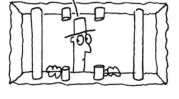

Ireland has the highest birth rate in the EU.

The phrase **"HE DIGS WITH HIS RIGHT/LEFT FOOT,"** denoting one's religion, originated in Ulster, where Catholics generally used a spade with a lug on the left and Protestants with one on the right.

The Conor Pass in Co. Kerry is the highest mountain pass in Ireland.

Ireland's **OLDEST NEWSPAPER** is the *Belfast News Letter* which was founded in 1737.

MAGPIES and Oliver Cromwell first arrived in Ireland around the same time and both landed in Wexford. Because of this, many people directly linked the birds with the invaders and believed Ireland would never be free of the English until we were rid of the magpies.

DAMN MAGPIES!

The lion that originally appeared in the **METRO-GOLDWYN-MAYER** logo was called "Slats" and was born in Dublin Zoo in 1919.

In the seventeenth century, Youghal council, Co. Cork, introduced a fine of £50 for deflowering the daughter of an alderman.

HOW MUCH WOULD IT BE IF I DEFLOWERED YOU TWICE?

In the early 1900s, **ALOIS HITLER**, half brother of Adolf Hitler, worked in the Shelbourne Hotel, Dublin.

Dominic West, the actor who played Detective **JIMMY McNULTY** in the television series *The Wire*, was educated at Trinity College, Dublin.

ST. OLIVER PLUNKETT'S head is on display in St. Peter's Church in Drogheda, Co. Louth. Some of the rest of his body is in Bath in England and the remainder is in Germany.

Rosslare in Co. Wexford is the sunniest town in Ireland, with 4.3 hours of sunshine per day.

According to international death rates (per thousand per annum), an Irish person is **FOUR TIMES** more likely to die in a given year than someone from the United Arab Emirates.

FINGALIAN was a language of Old English and Nordic origins that was spoken in the Fingal area of Dublin until the 1800s.

Since 2004, 150,000 **POLISH PEOPLE** have immigrated to Ireland and there are now more Polish speakers than Irish speakers in the country.

ICELAND was first settled by a group of Irish monks known as "The Papar."

The life expectancy for a woman in Ireland is 80.88 years.

BILLY THE BOWL was a legless murderer who got around Dublin in a tin bowl in the late eighteenth century. He turned from begging to robbery and murder and was eventually hanged in 1786.

When **MUHAMMAD ALI** fought Al Lewis in Croke Park in 1972, he was so desperate for a pee at the end of the tenth round that he launched a sustained attack on his opponent and finished him off in the eleventh.

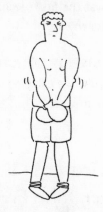

In 1973 the IRA landed a **HELICOPTER** in the exercise yard of Mountjoy Prison and rescued their chief-of-staff, Joe Tierney.

There are 120 recognised saints buried in the church graveyard of St. Eanna on the Aran Island of **INISHMORE**.

JACK KELLY, father of Irish-American actress and later princess, Grace Kelly, was the first person ever to win three Olympic gold medals for rowing.

The Church of Ireland **BISHOP OF RAPHOE**, Philip Twysden, was shot dead while carrying out a robbery on a stagecoach in London in 1752.

Beatle George Harrison's grandfather, John French, was born in Co. Wexford.

Until recently, there was a law on Ireland's statute books making it illegal to enhance **PROFITS ON COFFEE SALES** by mixing it with sheep dung.

Ireland has more **MOBILE PHONES** per capita than any other country in Europe.

There are 46 rivers in Dublin.

BRAM STOKER, the Irish author of *Dracula*, never visited eastern Europe in his entire lifetime.

When **MARY McALEESE** replaced Mary Robinson as Irish President, it became the first time in the world that one female president had succeeded another.

In the seventeenth century the British paid a £20 **BOUNTY** for every priest caught by a bounty hunter.

The **WESTLINK BRIDGE** across Dublin's River Liffey, which handles 21,000 vehicles a day, is the busiest bridge in Europe.

Croghan-Kinsella was the site of Ireland's only **GOLD RUSH**, in 1795, when a nugget was found in river gravel on the mountain. Three thousand ounces of gold were found before the gold was exhausted.

The highest ever **TEMPERATURE** recorded in Ireland was 33.3°C at Kilkenny Castle on June 26, 1887.

TODAY IT WILL BE TURTY TREE AND A TURD DEGREES IN IRELAND

Ceide Fields in Co. Mayo was the site of the largest known **STONE AGE COMMUNITY** in Europe, with as many as five thousand inhabitants at its peak.

The Bog of Allen is almost 1,000 square km in size.

Dublin's North **BULL WALL** was designed by Captain William Bligh, he of the infamous *Mutiny on the Bounty*.

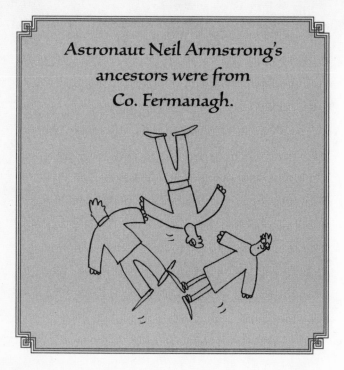

Astronaut Neil Armstrong's ancestors were from Co. Fermanagh.

The **SMALLEST CHURCH** in Ireland is St. Gobhans at Portbradden in Co. Antrim, measuring just 3 m by 1.8 m.

In Irish law, 14,500 Acts pre-date the Act of Union of 1801.

One of the few survivors of the famous Russian uprising or mutiny on the Battleship Potemkin in 1905, was **IVAN BESHOFF**, who made it to Dublin and opened the city's famous Beshoffs fish and chip shop, which is still in operation today.

CONEY ISLAND in New York was named after a tiny island off Sligo by an Irish captain, Peter O'Connor, in the eighteenth century.

The Rotunda in Dublin, opened in 1745, was the world's first purpose-built maternity hospital.

The **UNION JACK** contains a red saltire or diagonal cross, called St. Patrick's Cross, representing Ireland.

Up to the 1920s, couples in Teltown, Co. Meath could get **MARRIED** simply by walking towards each other.

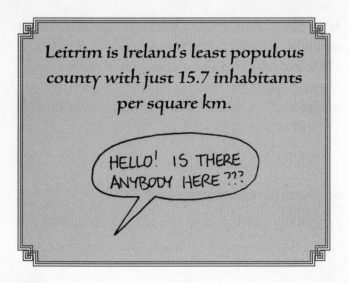

Leitrim is Ireland's least populous county with just 15.7 inhabitants per square km.

HELLO! IS THERE ANYBODY HERE ???

CAHIRCIVEEN CATHOLIC CHURCH, Co. Kerry, is the only one in Ireland named after a layman—Daniel O'Connell.

Cement was invented in 1789 by Bryan Higgins from Co. Sligo.

Ireland is more **DENSELY POPULATED** than the United States and Russia.

At the peak of Fr. Theobald Mathew's Temperance Movement around 1850, over three million Irish people had taken **"THE PLEDGE,"** i.e. not to drink alcohol again.

Cornelscourt, Co. Dublin, was Ireland's first **SHOPPING CENTRE**. It opened in 1966.

There are over 40,000 basalt columns in The Giant's Causeway in Co. Antrim.

The first action of the Easter 1916 **RISING** took place in Co. Laois, not Dublin, when Volunteers blew up a section of railway track on April 23, one day before a shot was fired in the capital.

The **HELL FIRE CLUB** on Montpelier Hill, south Dublin, was originally the scene of orgies of drinking, gambling, and wanton sex among wealthy young individuals of the late 1700s. The motto of this group was "Do as you will."

The **OLD MILITARY ROAD** in Co. Wicklow was built by the British to help fight Michael Dwyer, who had been successfully fighting a guerilla war against them in the hills for over six years after the 1798 rebellion.

Irish writers have been awarded the Nobel Prize for Literature four times: Yeats, Shaw, Beckett, and Heaney.

Although Irish, the **DUKE OF WELLINGTON**, who defeated Napoleon at Waterloo, was not proud of his roots and is reputed to have said, "Being born in a stable does not make one a horse."

The antlers of the now extinct **IRISH ELK** could measure as much as twelve feet across.

THOMAS MOORE'S statue in College Green, Dublin shares a traffic island with a public toilet. The statue's nickname is "The meeting of the waters," thus honouring his famous poem and the nearby public convenience.

Co. Cork is nine times the size of Co. Louth.

A **KELPIE** is a supernatural water horse, believed to haunt the lakes of Ireland, which can transform itself into a handsome man to lure women into the water, drown them, and eat them.

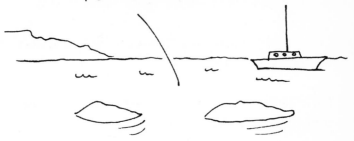

I'M HAVING SOME FRIENDS OVER FOR DINNER...

Ireland was hit by its worst ever **STORM** in 1839 when wind speed reached over 201 kph, killing hundreds of people.

The earliest reference to Dublin is in the writings of the Greek cartographer **PTOLEMY** in 140, who called the settlement "Eblana."

The sub-atomic term **"ELECTRON"** was introduced by Irish physicist George Johnstone Stoney in 1891.

SUB ATOMIC
ELECTRON

In Irish mythology, **ACHTLAND** was a mortal woman who could not find a human male to satisfy her sexual needs, so she took a giant from the race of Tuatha Dé Danann as her mate.

*If you hear a banshee's wail,
someone's about to kick the bucket.*

When Irish scientist Mary Ward was killed by a steam-powered automobile driven by her cousin in 1869, she officially became the world's first **ROAD TRAFFIC ACCIDENT** victim.

MAKE SURE... THAT... THEY... KNOW... I WAS... THE FIRST!

Ireland is the twentieth-largest island in the world. Greenland is No. 1.

The first European to set foot on American soil was not Christopher Columbus but Irishman **PATRICK MAGUIRE**, who was a member of the crew.

The first **POTATOES** in Europe were grown by Sir Walter Raleigh in 1596 on his estate in Youghal, Co. Cork.

Irish-American actor **AUDIE MURPHY**, who was a top Hollywood star of the fifties, was the most decorated soldier of World War II, receiving twenty-eight citations for bravery, including the Medal of Honor.

HOW AM I SUPPOSED TO FIGHT WITH THESE THINGS

The man who designed the O'Connell Monument in Dublin, **JOHN HENRY FOLEY**, also designed the Albert Memorial in London.

There are 628 known megalithic tombs in Ireland.

The **PASSWORD** for George Washington's troops in Boston in 1776 was "St. Patrick."

Dublin's first **BUS ROUTE** was started by the Clondalkin Omnibus Company in 1919. The vehicle was a horse-drawn wooden structure resting on a 5-ton chassis.

BET IT STILL GOT IN TO TOWN QUICKER.

In 1795 a Belfast doctor and poet, William Drennar, was the first to coin the phrase **"THE EMERALD ISLE."**

The Irish Wolfhound is the tallest dog breed in the world.

LOUGH DERG (meaning "red lake") in Co. Donegal gets its name from the legend of St. Patrick killing a serpent in the lake, the blood turning the water red.

Takabuti, the first **MUMMY** to be seen publicly outside of Egypt, was displayed in Belfast in 1831 and is still on display at the Ulster Museum.

The Irish theologian and philosopher **JOHANNES SCOTUS ERIUGENA** (815–877) was once asked by King Charles the Bald of France, "What separates a drunkard from an Irishman?" to which Johannes replied, "Only a table."

I MAY BE DRUNK BUT AT LEAST I'M NOT A BALDY FECKER LIKE YOU

Famous Irish writer and wit **OSCAR WILDE'S** full name was Oscar Fingal O'Flahertie Wills Wilde.

During the famine in 1847, the **CHOCTAW INDIANS** from southeast US raised $710 for famine relief, the equivalent today of about one million dollars.

Arthur Guinness had 21 children.

The longest complete **DROUGHT** in Ireland was recorded in Limerick, from April 3 to May 10, 1938, just 37 days.

Cork gets its name from the Irish word corcach meaning "marsh."

There are actually two **O'CONNELL BRIDGES** in Dublin: one spans the Liffey and the other crosses the pond in St. Stephen's Green.

A law originally on the Irish statute books made it illegal for a student to walk through **TRINITY COLLEGE** without wearing a sword.

Ireland's most northerly point is **INISHTRAHULL ISLAND**, 7 km north of the Donegal coast.

In 1840 only half the Irish population could read or write.

Trinity College **LIBRARY** is legally entitled to a copy of every book published in Great Britain and Ireland. The library currently has 4.5 million books.

Being awarded the **FREEDOM OF DUBLIN** gives you the right to graze sheep on College Green.

Ireland has had four major **CURRENCY** changes in forty years: the pound sterling (pounds, shillings, and pence), replaced by the decimal pound in 1971, replaced by the Irish pound in 1978, replaced by the euro in 2002.

A **MERROW** is the Celtic equivalent of a mermaid, said to reveal their naked upper bodies to young men to lure them into the sea.

THE WATER'S FREEZIN'?

The 1964 musical **MY FAIR LADY** was based on Irishman George Bernard Shaw's play *Pygmalion*.

The Great **STALACTITE** in Doolin Cave, Co. Clare, is the world's largest free-hanging stalactite.

EDWARD BRUCE, brother of the more famous Robert, King of Scotland, was once crowned King of Ireland.

The Academy Award's **OSCAR** statuette was designed by Cedric Gibbons, who was born in Dublin.

According to an ancient Irish superstition, having a haircut on Good Friday will prevent you from getting headaches for a year.

KATHERINE PLUNKET, an aristocrat from Co. Louth, was the oldest Irish person ever. She died in 1932, aged 111.

Only 20 percent of Irish primary school teachers are male.

Irish scientist John Joly from Offaly was the first man to use **RADIATION** to treat cancerous tumours.

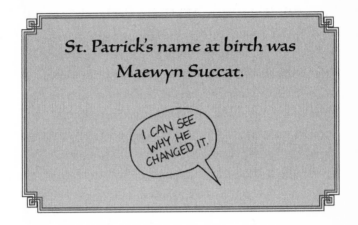

There were about 120 Irish passengers on the **TITANIC**, most of whom died. One Irish girl, called Anna Kelly, who had gone on deck to find out what had happened, survived and later became a nun.

The correct title for Irishman Jonathan Swift's famous novel **GULLIVER'S TRAVELS** is *Travels into Several Remote Nations of the World, in Four Parts. By Lemuel Gulliver, First a Surgeon, and then a Captain of Several Ships.*

The longest **HUNGER STRIKE** in world history was by nine republicans in Cork prison in 1920. They went 94 days without food.

Leitrim only got its first set of traffic lights in 2003.

NOW ALL WE NEED IS SOME TRAFFIC!

According to *The Times History of the War*, both sides ceased fire briefly during the 1916 Rising to allow the St. Stephen's Green **PARK KEEPER**, Joseph Kearney, to feed the wide variety of waterfowl in the park.

Torr Head in Co. Antrim is just 23 km from Scotland.

In a 2002 BBC Global Service poll, "A Nation Once Again" was voted the **WORLD'S MOST POPULAR SONG**.

It was when flying over Ireland in a plane that **JOHNNY CASH** was inspired to write the song "Forty Shades of Green."

THINK IM GOING TO BE AIRSICK...

The first ever **ST. PATRICK'S DAY PARADE** was held in New York on March 17, 1762 by Irish soldiers who were serving in the British Army.

In hurling, a sliotar can travel at speeds of up to 150 kph.

Louis Brennan from Castlebar invented the **STEERABLE TORPEDO** and the world's first trials took place in Crosshaven, Co. Cork.

The body that preceded the Irish Censorship Board was called "The Committee on **EVIL LITERATURE**."

Bushmills in Co. Antrim is the oldest **WHISKEY DISTILLERY** in the world still in operation. It is 401 years old.

Ireland's first cinema, The Volta on Mary Street, Dublin, opened in 1909.

When J.M. Synge's play **THE PLAYBOY OF THE WESTERN WORLD** premiered in the Abbey Theatre in Dublin in 1907, there were riots as the play was believed to have "cast a slight on the virtue of Irish womanhood."

Although the game of polo originated in Persia, it was first played in Europe in Limerick in 1868.

LADS... THAT'S NOT FOR BATIN' EACH OTHER WITH

Thirteen counties have yet to register an **ALL IRELAND SENIOR FOOTBALL CHAMPIONSHIP** win: Wicklow, Carlow, Monaghan, Longford, Westmeath, Laois, Kilkenny, Waterford, Clare, Sligo, Leitrim, Fermanagh, and Antrim.

The last survivor of the 1789 **MUTINY ON THE BOUNTY** was John Adams from Co. Derry.

In the 1970s Irish musician **BOB GELDOF** worked in an abattoir, a pea canning factory, and as a road navvy.

Between 500–800 **IRELAND'S MONASTIC SETTLEMENTS** had the status in Europe in educational terms that Harvard, Yale, or Oxford enjoy today.

LORD EDWARD FITZGERALD, who was one of the leaders of the 1798 rebellion, was also an officially adopted Chief of the Huron Tribe of North American Indians.

Up until 1996, any visitor to the Hideout Pub in Kilcullen, Co. Kildare, could view the arm that brought legendary Irish world champion boxer Dan Donnelly such success. After he died in 1820 his body was stolen by graverobbers for medical research and eventually a travelling salesman purchased the **SEVERED SKELETAL ARM** and sold it to the pub's owner who put it on display in a glass case.

Ireland has more dogs per capita than any other country in Europe.

NEWGRANGE passage tomb was built five hundred years before the Great Pyramid at Giza.

"Gentleman" **JIM CORBETT**, the famous Irish-American boxer, reputedly soaked his bandages in Plaster of Paris before a fight.

The green, white, and orange of the **IRISH TRICOLOUR** was inspired by the red, white, and blue of the French tricolour after Thomas Francis Meagher had visited Paris during a period of revolution.

VIVA LES PADDIES

A statue of William of Orange that once stood opposite Trinity College was blown up in 1946. It was the last **EQUESTRIAN STATUE** in Dublin.

SHEELA NA GIGS are ancient stone carvings of a female figure openly displaying her genitals, often found on church walls around Ireland. There are over one hundred in Ireland and they are thought to have warded off evil spirits.

Beatle John Lennon's grandfather, Jack Lennon, and grandmother, Mary Maguire, were Irish.

Galway-born actor **PETER O'TOOLE** has been nominated eight times for an Oscar as Best Actor in a Leading Role, giving him a unique record as the most nominated actor never to have won the award.

In 2005, there was one pub for every 350 people in Ireland.

The hypodermic **SYRINGE** was invented by Dubliner Dr. Francis Rynd in 1845 and the first injection in the world was administered at the Meath Hospital.

LET ME TELL YOU WHERE YOU CAN STICK YOUR FANCY SYRINGE!

PAUL McCARTNEY'S father and grandfather were born in Ireland and his grandfather's character was portrayed by Irish actor Wilfrid Brambell in the movie *A Hard Day's Night*.

Fishamble Street in Dublin's Temple Bar was the location of the first performance of **HANDEL'S *MESSIAH*** in April 1742.

The first Irish Constitution was signed in Room 112 of the Shelbourne Hotel, Dublin, in 1922.

An Irishwoman, Jennie Hodgers from Co. Louth, served for the duration of the US Civil War disguised **AS A MAN**.

WHAT WAS IT THAT GAVE ME AWAY SIR??

GEORGE BEST Belfast City Airport is the only airport in the world named after a footballer.

If the Belfast-built ship *TITANIC* had hit the iceberg head-on, in all probability it would have stayed afloat.

NOW HE TELLS US...

Legislation was introduced to **LEGALISE CONDOMS** in Ireland in 1979, making them available to over-18s on prescription. This was two years older than the legal age at which you could marry.

Ireland's coastline measures 1,448 km.

In 2008 an **ORANGUTAN** escaped its enclosure and spent an hour wandering around Dublin Zoo.

The only reptile species native to Ireland is the **VIVIPAROUS LIZARD**, found mainly in the southwest.

The Irish Proclamation was one of the first such documents in the world to recognize the **EQUALITY** of men and women.

NO, YOU'RE NOT PAID LESS
BECAUSE YOU'RE A WOMAN!
WE'RE JUST PAID MORE
CAUSE WE'RE MEN.

The Irish are the biggest per capita consumers of tea in the world.

The windows in the Bank of Ireland, College Green were bricked up to avoid paying "window tax." It was this tax that allegedly gave rise to the term **"DAYLIGHT ROBBERY."**

The **GUINNESS BOOK OF RECORDS** came into existence because Sir Hugh Beaver, MD of Guinness, got into an argument while hunting in Wexford over which was the fastest game bird in Europe, the golden plover or the grouse.

St. Columcille is the patron saint of bookbinders and poets.

YOLA is a now-extinct Germanic language that was spoken in south Wexford up to the mid-nineteenth century.

The **WETTEST DAY** ever recorded somewhere in Ireland was at Cloore Lake, Co. Kerry on September 18, 1993, when 243.5 mm of rain fell.

The **HAROLD'S CROSS** area in Dublin is said to derive its name from the name of a gallows which was erected in the fourteenth century on the spot now occupied by Harold's Cross Park. It continued to be a place of execution until the eighteenth century.

THIS PLACE IS DEADLY!

Although a pacifist, in 1815 **DANIEL O'CONNELL** shot and killed John D'Esterre, a member of Dublin Corporation, in a duel.

HMMM. SORRY ABOUT THAT.

Adolf Hitler had a contingency plan to **INVADE IRELAND** codenamed "Operation Emerald."

2,000 men were (legally) executed in Ireland in the nineteenth century.

CORK HARBOUR is the world's second largest natural harbour, after Sydney Harbour in Australia.

There are sixty-four towns in Ireland beginning with the prefix **"BALLY."**

In 1968, a 1,000-year-old block of cheese was found **PRESERVED** in a bog in Tipperary.

The coach used by The Queen of England at the State Opening of Parliament is called the **IRISH STATE COACH** because the original was built in 1851 by the Lord Mayor of Dublin, John Reynolds, who was also a coachbuilder.

In 2006, there were 2,494 more women than men in Ireland.

In the mid-seventeenth century, Oliver Cromwell ordered the burning of all **HARPS** found in Ireland.

THE PALE was an area in the twelfth century that included Dublin, Meath, Louth, and part of Kildare. Anyone from outside this was considered to be a bit of a savage, thus "Beyond the pale."

Since its founding in 1968, **KNOCK MARRIAGE BUREAU** in Co. Mayo has been instrumental in bringing about almost one thousand marriages.

Irish women got the vote in 1928.

The last person to be publicly executed in the UK was Irishman **MICHAEL BARRETT** who was wrongly hanged for the Clerkenwell bombings of 1867.

The Roman name for Ireland, **HIBERNIA**, comes from the Latin *hibernus*, which means "wintry."

The **LARGEST FARM** in history was owned by Samuel McCaughey from Co. Ballymena. It was in Australia's Northern Territory and was bigger than Northern Ireland.

Ronald Reagan hushed up his **IRISH ROOTS** before he was elected president of the US because he was afraid it would turn some voters against him.

In 1800, the population of Ireland was twice that of the United States.

According to Limerick-born actor Richard Harris, the mansion he owned in England was **HAUNTED** by an eight-year-old boy who he could hear running around, banging doors, and generally keeping him awake. He managed to placate the spirit somewhat by having a nursery, complete with toys and games, built in a tower of the mansion.

Enya is Ireland's most successful solo artist, with sales of over 70 million albums.

The giant sea-stack at **DUN BRISTE**, Co. Mayo was connected to the land by an arch as recently as 1393. When it collapsed, the people living there had to be rescued by climbing across the newly created chasm on ships' ropes. No one returned to the top of Dun Briste until the twentieth century.

St. John's Cathedral in Limerick has the tallest spire in Ireland at 94 m.

There was once a town with nine named streets on the island of Bannow in Co. Wexford, built in the twelfth century. In the seventeenth century the channel separating the island from the mainland silted up and the shifting sands eventually completely buried the town, which became known for a time as the **IRISH HERCULANEUM**. The only indication of its existence are the ruins of a Norman church still visible on what is now a peninsula.

At the **ITALIA '90 WORLD CUP**, Ireland reached the quarter-finals having scored only two goals in five matches.

♪ ♫ ♪♪ ♪♪ ♪ YOU'LL NEVER
BEAT THE IRISH
(UNTIL THE QUARTER FINALS)

The person who "blew his mind out in a car" in the famous Beatles song **"A DAY IN THE LIFE,"** was Tara Brown, an heir to a Guinness fortune. He is buried in a grave on the shores of Luggula Lake in Co. Wicklow

Taoiseach Jack Lynch, discussing the ban on condoms, once said that he'd decided to "put the issue on the **LONG FINGER**."

The statue of **QUEEN VICTORIA** outside the Queen Victoria Building in Sydney, Australia once stood outside Leinster House, Dublin.

The name **CURRAGH** literally means "racecourse." The first recorded race took place at the Curragh in 1727, although it's thought races have been held there for 2,000 years.

In Ireland the life expectancy for a man is 75.44 years.

Leopardstown in Dublin derives its name from the Irish, *Baile an Lobhair*, meaning **"TOWN OF THE LEPERS."**

Laytown Races in Co. Meath is the only official Irish race meeting run on a beach.

Shane McGowan of The Pogues first played with a 1977 English punk band called **THE NIPPLE ERECTORS**.

Despite being less than 100 km from Wales, which has one of the world's richest coal fields, Ireland is virtually devoid of coal.

Officially, a **FREEMAN OR FREEWOMAN** of Dublin must own a bow, a coat of mail, a helmet, and a sword.

The **RED HAND** on the Ulster flag comes from a legend about a boat race between rival chieftains, the winner being awarded the kingship of Ulster. The victor would be the one whose hand first touched the shore. Losing as he approached the land, the chieftain Heremon O'Neill so loved Ulster that he cut off his hand and threw the bloodied appendage ashore, so claiming victory.

EW!
TAKE IT —
IF YOU WANT
IT THAT BAD!

Moles, common in Britain, are absent from Ireland.

The interior of the largest church in Ireland, **ST. PATRICK'S CATHEDRAL**, Dublin, could fit sideways into St. Peter's in Rome with 70 m to spare.

PADRAIG HARRINGTON is the only southern Irishman ever to win a golfing major. And he's won three. Fred Daly from Northern Ireland won one in 1947.

At the 1908 Olympics, Irish athletes competing for other countries won 23 medals, including eight golds.

OFFALY is the only county to have won a GAA All Star in every position in both hurling and football.

DRACULA, written by Dubliner Bram Stoker in 1897, has never once been out of print.

The **LONGEST DISTANCE** you can travel in a straight line in Ireland is from a point on the northeast coast of Co. Antrim (to the east of Ballycastle) to a point on the southwest coast of Co. Cork, (to the east of Schull), a distance of 468 km.

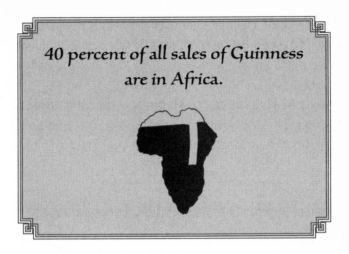

40 percent of all sales of Guinness are in Africa.

The Irish **CROWN JEWELS** were stolen in 1907 and the main suspect was Francis Shackleton, brother of the famed polar explorer, Ernest, although he was never charged.

U2 were originally called **THE LARRY MULLEN BAND** and used to practise in Larry's kitchen.

Muckross Lake, near Killarney in Co. Kerry, is reputed to be the **DEEPEST LAKE** in Ireland at 64 m.

Divorce was legal in Ireland until 1937.

The double-earpiece **STETHOSCOPE** was invented by Wexford doctor Arthur Leared.

Balbriggan was once famous worldwide for producing **MEN'S LONG JOHNS**, giving the male underwear the name "Balbriggans," a term used several times by nineteenth century Wild West characters played by John Wayne.

MOUNTJOY SQUARE is supposedly the only square in Dublin that is actually square.

Hurling has been played in Ireland for at least 2,000 years.

Multiple Eurovision winner **JOHNNY LOGAN** played Gaelic football for the Louth minors.

HOLD ME NOW

Two countries became Republics in 1949, Ireland and China.

The national symbol of Ireland is not the shamrock, but the Celtic **HARP**.

In 1895, **MICHAEL CLEARY** from Clonmel was tried for the murder of his wife Bridget, who he had burned to death because he believed she had been replaced by a fairy changeling. He was found guilty of manslaughter.

Director James Cameron was unhappy with the performance of Gaelic Storm, the Irish band who appear in the film **TITANIC**, when they first played on set. They explained that when he'd seen them play live they'd been pissed. Cameron immediately ordered more beer to be brought on set until the band were sozzled enough to perform to his liking.

KEEP DRINKING LADS!

Danny la Rue, the famous drag artist, was born Daniel Patrick Carroll in Cork city.

Although **NEWGRANGE** is over 5,000 years old, some of the markings inside were later discovered to be graffiti, probably made by plundering Vikings around 750.

Lough Corrib in Co. Galway has an **ISLAND** for every day of the year—365 in total.

The term **"NOSEY PARKER"** originated with a British soldier, Edward Parker, stationed in Co. Laois, who had an unfortunate tumour on his protuberance so that his nose almost reached his chin.

In ancient Irish Brehon Law there were seven forms of **MARRIAGE**. The seventh form, a seventh degree union, was a one-night stand.

SWORDS in north Co. Dublin, a small village in the 1960s, is now the eighth largest town in the Republic of Ireland.

The two mountains on the Cork-Kerry border, called **THE PAPS**, were believed to be the breasts of the ancient fertility goddess Anu. Each of the Paps has a large nipple-like cairn on its summit.

The first ever colour picture on the front of *The Irish Times* showed **STEPHEN ROCHE** on the Tour de France winner's podium in 1987.

Field Marshall **HORATIO KITCHENER**, famous as the face of the World War I recruitment posters bearing the pointing finger and the slogan, "Your Country Needs You," was from Co. Kerry.

The internationally regarded **OPERA**, *The Bohemian Girl*, was composed by Dubliner William Balfe.

The song "It's a Long Way to Tipperary" was written by two Englishmen, Jack Judge and Harry Williams.

The 2,630-metre high **MOUNT CREAN** in Antarctica is named after Kerryman and polar explorer, Tom Crean.

DRINKING CHOCOLATE was invented in the late 1600s by Sir Hans Sloane from Co. Down who was president of the Royal College of Physicians.

During Ireland's **ICE AGE** (which ended 10,000 years ago) every piece of land above a line from north Kerry to Waterford was completely covered in ice.

Patrick is the 42nd most popular first name in the US.

In 1914, the **GUINNESS** brewery at St. James's Gate, Dublin, was the largest brewery in the world.

The Liffey was once so polluted with sewage that writer and playwright **BRENDAN BEHAN** described the annual Liffey Swim as, "Going through the motions."

The **LAST WOMAN HANGED** in Ireland was Annie Walsh, aged 31, who was executed in 1925 for having murdered her husband with an axe.

FASTNET ROCK is not the most southerly point of Ireland. This title belongs to Little Fastnet, a much smaller rock 30 m to the south.

OVER HERE!

The Transport Workers' Union of America was founded by a Kerry republican activist, **MIKE QUILL**, in 1934.

The world's most popular **SHORTHAND** system, Gregg Shorthand, was invented by Irishman John Robert Gregg from Co. Monaghan.

The driest year on record in Ireland was 1887.

Irish-American **JOHN F. KENNEDY** is the only Catholic ever to be elected president of the US.

The border between the Republic and Northern Ireland is 360 km long.

Renowned Co. Clare writer **EDNA O'BRIEN'S** first three books were banned because of their sexual content.

BAILEYS IRISH CREAM, launched in 1974, was the first cream liqueur in the world.

There are three **UNESCO** world heritage sites on the island of Ireland: Brú na Bóinne, Skellig Michael, and the Giant's Causeway. The Rock of Cashel is under consideration.

MAYBE IF IT HAD A ROOF?

When the **VIKINGS** firmly established themselves in Waterford in 914, it became Ireland's first city.

The first successful **FLIGHT ACROSS THE ATLANTIC** from east to west was completed on April 13, 1928 by Irishman James Fitzmaurice, taking off from Baldonnel Aerodrome, Dublin and landing on Greenly Island, Quebec, Canada.

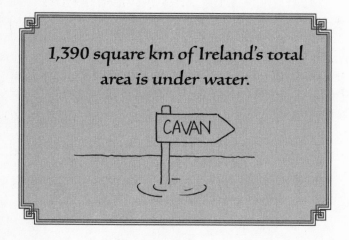

1,390 square km of Ireland's total area is under water.

CAVAN

When the British were handing over power to **MICHAEL COLLINS** in 1922, Lord Lieutenant FitzAlan remarked that Collins had arrived seven minutes late for the ceremony. Collins replied, "We've been waiting over seven hundred years, you can have the extra seven minutes."

The term **"YAHOO,"** nowadays meaning a yobbo or hooligan, was coined by Irish writer Jonathan Swift as the name of the race of sub-humans or de-evolved humans in *Gulliver's Travels*.

Three Irish counties have no cinema: Cavan, Laois, and Roscommon.

IRISH COFFEE was invented by Joseph Sheridan, the head chef at Shannon International Airport in the 1940s.

GEORGE BARRINGTON was Ireland and Britain's most infamous pickpocket in the early nineteenth century. He once picked a snuff box from Russian Count Orlov worth £30,000 (millions by today's standards).

HARRY GEORGE FERGUSON, one of the founders of the international tractor company Massey Ferguson, made the first powered flight in Ireland, travelling 118.5 m in a monoplane he had built himself.

Thomas John Barnardo, the founder of the famous children's charity, **BARNARDO'S**, was from Dublin.

In 2006, the US National Retail Federation reported that 93 million Americans planned to wear green on St. Patrick's Day.

The most popular Irish **SURNAME** in the US is Moore, in ninth place.

In 2004 Ireland became the first country in the world to introduce a comprehensive **SMOKING BAN** in all workplaces.

As of 2009, Ireland's top ten **RICHEST** people have over €8 billion between them.

Shelta is a language spoken by many of the Irish Traveller community.

In 1871, the murderer of bank official William Glass in Newtownstewart, Co. Tyrone, turned out to be T.H. Montgomery, the **DETECTIVE** who was investigating the case.

You could fit Ireland into the US 130 times.

Irish nationalist **CONSTANCE MARKIEWICZ** was the first woman to be elected to the British House of Commons.

Navan-born **PIERCE BROSNAN'S** first movie role was in the 1980 London gangster film, *The Long Good Friday*, in which he appeared in just a handful of brief scenes playing the role of "1st Irishman."

RONAN KEATING is in the *Guinness Book of Records* for being the only artist ever to have thirty consecutive top ten singles in the UK chart, out-scoring even the Beatles and Elvis.

15,000 years ago you could have walked from Ireland to Scotland over a land bridge.

JAMESON is the top selling Irish whiskey in the world.

The first **IMMIGRANT** to officially enter the United States through the Ellis Island facility in New York was a young Irish girl named Annie Moore. A statue of her marks both her departure point in Cobh, Co. Cork and at Ellis Island.

The largest **STONE CIRCLE** in Ireland is at Lough Gur in Co. Limerick. It is 50 m in diameter and has 113 standing stones, the largest of which is 4 m high and weighs 40 tons. It was built 4,000 years ago.

Fastnet Island used to be known as **IRELAND'S TEARDROP** as it was often the last piece of their homeland that emigrants would ever see.

Legendary Belfast footballer, George Best played for nine different football clubs, including Cork Celtic.

I'M HERE TO SEE OUR GEORGE PLAY... WHICH TEAM IS HE ON?

PATRICIA is the second most popular female given name in the US. Mary is first.

Daniel O'Connell was once the Lord Mayor of Dublin.

The British built fifty **MARTELLO TOWERS** around Ireland to watch for an invasion by Napoleon that never came.

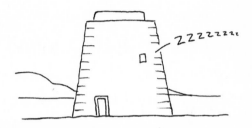

A large percentage of **ICELAND'S** population are the descendants of Irish slaves brought there by Norsemen in the ninth century.

ALCOCK AND BROWN made the first non-stop transatlantic flight in June 1919, crash-landing in a bog near Clifden, Co. Galway which, from the sky, looked like a level green field. Both airmen survived.

THANK YOU FOR FLYING ALCOCK & BROWN. WE HOPE YOU HAD A PLEASANT FLIGHT...

Famous director Stanley Kubrick's highly regarded movie, **BARRY LYNDON**, was shot mostly around Powerscourt House, Co. Wicklow, with the area playing itself, England, and Prussia.

Powerscourt Waterfall in Co. Wicklow is Ireland's highest waterfall at 121 m.

Kilkenny's hurling team are known as **THE CATS** from the phrase "to fight like a Kilkenny cat," originating from stories of how people used to make cats fight each other to the death, often with their tails tied together.

The **LUSITANIA**, regarded as the second most famous maritime disaster after the Titanic, was sunk by a German U-Boat just off The Old Head of Kinsale, Co. Cork on May 7, 1915 with the loss of 1,198 lives.

Two **DOGS**, the property of a first class passenger, survived the sinking of the *Titanic*.

John Jesus Flanagan from Co. Limerick, competing for the US, won the **OLYMPIC HAMMER-THROWING** gold medal at the 1900, 1904, and 1908 Olympic Games.

AH JESUS JOHN WILL YE WATCH WHERE YOU THROW THAT BLEEDIN' THING!

BONO reputedly got his name from a hearing aid shop in North Earl Street, Dublin called Bonavox, which literally translates as "good voice." He subsequently shortened it to Bono.

*Enya's real name is
Eithne Patricia Ní Bhraonáin.*

The town of **BUTTEVANT** in Co. Cork is believed to derive its name from the war cry of the Barry family, "Boutez-en-Avant" meaning "strike forward."

The Marxist revolutionary Che Guevara's full name was **CHE GUEVARA LYNCH**, as both his parents were of Irish-Spanish descent.

Hollywood actor **MEL GIBSON'S** first name comes from St. Mel, a fifth-century Irish saint, while his middle name, Colm-Cille, comes from a sixth-century Irish saint.

The world's first **CHEESE & ONION** flavoured crisp was invented in 1954 by Joe "Spud" Murphy, founder of Tayto Crisps.

James Martin from Co. Down invented the world's first **EJECTOR SEAT** in 1945. The following year the first live test subject, Bernard Lynch, was launched into the air and landed safely.

Up to the early 1980s, a towering chimney stood on Shelbourne Road, Ballsbridge, Dublin across which was emblazoned a **HUGE SWASTIKA**. The chimney was part of The Swastika Laundry, which had operated there up to the late 1960s. The odd-looking landmark has since been demolished.

The name of the city of **TALLAGHT** is derived from "*támh leacht*," meaning "plague burial place."

Although **GREEN** is the colour most associated with Ireland, St. Patrick's cloak was actually blue and St. Patrick's Blue is the official colour of the Presidential Standard and on the coat of arms of Ireland.

In 1916, Irish polar explorer **ERNEST SHACKLETON** travelled 1,287 m from Antarctica in a small whale boat across towering polar seas to South Georgia Island to get help for his stranded crew. Shackleton and two of the men then crossed the mountains of South Georgia with just 15 m of rope for climbing to reach a whaling station. All his crew were eventually rescued.

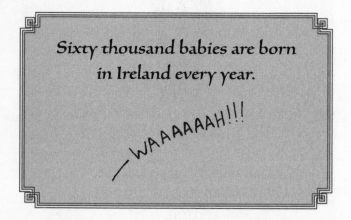

Sixty thousand babies are born in Ireland every year.

— WAAAAAAH!!!

The name **IRELAND** comes from the Celtic mother goddess Ériu, giving us Eire.

Murphy is the most common name in Ireland.

The lease on St. James's Gate Brewery, where Guinness is brewed, doesn't expire until the year 10759.

THIS IS A REALLY IMPORTANT BIT OF TRIVIA

feckin'
írísh
proverbs

An old Irish proverb goes, *Seachain an duine a bhíonn ina thost*, which means "Beware of the person of few words." And never a truer word was said. And with this unique collection of age-old Irish proverbs, supplied in the original Irish and in English, you'll never be short of a few wise words yourself.

So don't delay, because *Ní fhanann tráigh le éinne!* or in other words, "Time and tide waits for no man!"

Appearances

Is glas iad na cnoic i bhfad uainn.
Faraway hills are green.

Cuir síoda ar ghabhar ach is gabhar i gcónaí é.
You can put silk on a goat, but it's still a goat.

Is minic ubh mhór ag cearc bheag.
A small hen often has a large egg.

Is minic a rug cú mall ar ghiorria.
The slow hound often captures the hare.

Brevity

Más gearr é do scéal is greannmhar.
The shorter your story, the funnier.

An rud a théann i bhfad, téann sé i bhfuaire.
What drags on grows cold.

Boastfulness

Ná glac duine choíche ar a thuaraisc fhéin.
Never accept someone on their opinion of themselves.

An té is ciúine is é is buaine.
The silent one is the strongest one.

Character

Ní h-aithne go h-aontíos.
You won't know someone until you live with them.

Aithníonn ciaróg ciaróg eile.
One beetle recognizes another beetle.

Seachain an duine a bhíonn ina thost.
Beware of the person of few words.

Is minic a bhí fear maith i seanbhríste.
There's often a good man in old trousers.

Is dóigh le fear gan chiall gurb é féin fear na céille.
The man without sense thinks he is the sensible one.

Drochubh, drochéan.
A bad egg, a bad bird.

Bíonn caora dhubh ar an tréad is gile.
The whitest flock has a black sheep.

Children

Is mac do mhac go bpósfaidh sé. Ach is iníon d'iníon go dtéir i gcré.

A son is your son until he marries. But a daughter is forever.

An mháthair leis an mac agus an iníon leis an athair.

The mother takes sides with the son and the daughter with the father.

Commonsense

Ní haon ualach an chiall.

Sense is not a heavy burden.

Ná nocht d'fhiacla go bhféadair an greim do bhreith.

Don't bare your teeth unless you can bite.

Ná bac le mac an bhacaigh, agus ní bhacfaidh mac an bhacaigh leat.

Don't bother the beggar's son and the beggar's son won't bother you.

Confidentiality

Ní scéal rúin é más fios do thriúr é.
It isn't a secret if three know it.

Courage

Is teann gach madra gearr i ndoras a thí féin.
Every terrier is bold in its own doorway.

Glaonn gach coileach go dána ar a atrainn féin.
Every cock crows boldly in his own farmyard.

Death

Níl luibh nó leigheas in aghaidh an bhás.
There is no cure for death.

*Dá mbeifeá chomh láidir le crann darach, gheobhaidh an bás
an ceann is fearr ort.*
If you were as strong as an oak, death will still
vanquish you.

Discretion

*Má's maith leat síocháin, cairdeas agus moladh, éist, féach, is
fan balbh!*
If you want peace, friendship, and praise, listen, look,
and be dumb!

Is minic a bhris béal duine a shrón.
A man's mouth often broke his nose.

Bíonn cluasa ar na clathacha.
The fences have ears.

Ni théann cuileog san mbéal a bhíos dúnta.
A closed mouth catches no flies.

Beagán a rá agus é a rá go maith.
Say little but say it well.

Drinking

Roghnaigh do chuideachta sul a dtéann tú ag ól.
Choose your company before you go drinking.

Nuair a bhíonn an t-ól istigh, bíonn an chiall amuigh.
When drink is in, sense is out.

Sgéitheann fíon fírinne!
Wine reveals the truth!

Dá fheabhas é an t-ól is é an tart a dheireadh.
Good as drink is, it ends in thirst.

Is milis dá ól é ach is searbh dá íoc é.
Drinking is sweet, but paying for it is bitter.

Experience

Ag duine féin is fearr a fhios cá luíonn an bhróg air.
The wearer best knows where the shoe pinches.

Ní bhíonn an rath, ach mara mbíonn an smacht.
There is no prosperity unless there is discipline.

Is í an dias is troime is ísle a chromas a cheann.
The heaviest ear of grain bends its head the lowest.

Ní thagann ciall roimh aois.
Sense doesn't come before age.

Tar éis a thuigtear gach beart.
It's easy to be wise after the event.

Family

Is fearr beagán den ghaol ná mórán den charthanas.
A little kinship is better than a lot of charity.

Is treise dúchas ná oiliúint.
Instinct is stronger than upbringing.

Mol an páiste agus molann tú an mháthair.
Praise the child and you praise the mother.

Food

Is maith an t-anlann an t-ocras
Hunger is a good sauce.

Is fearr greim de choinín ná dhá ghreim de chat.
One bite of a rabbit is better than two bites of a cat.

Is fearr bothán biamhar ná caisleán gortach.
A cabin with plenty of food is better than a hungry castle.

Friendship

Má bhíonn tú ar lorg cara gan locht, beidh tú gan chara go deo.
If you seek a friend without fault, you will be friendless
forever.

Is maith an scáthán súil charad.
A friend's eye is a good mirror.

Aithnítear cara i gcruatán.
A friend is known in hardship.

Generosity

Ní dheachaigh fial riamh go hIfreann.
A generous person never went to Hell.

Gossip

Inis do Mháire i gcogar é, is inseoidh Máire do phobal é.
Tell it to Mary in a whisper and Mary will tell it to
the parish.

An té a thabharfas scéal chugat tabharfaidh sé dhá scéal uait.
He who brings a story to you will take two stories
from you.

Bíonn siúlach scéalach.
Travellers have tales to tell.

Guilt

Is minic a bhí ciúin ciontach.
Silence often denotes guilt.

Hastiness

Mol an lá um thráthnóna.
Don't praise the day until evening.

Ná tabhair breith ar an chéad scéal.
Never judge on first opinions.

Health

Is fearr an sláinte ná an táinte.
Health is better than wealth.

*An té nach leigheasann im nó uisce beatha, níl aon
leigheas air.*
If whiskey or butter won't cure someone, nothing will.

I dtosach na h-aicíde is fusa í a leigheas.
Illness is easiest cured at the start.

Maireann croí éadrom i bhfad.
A light heart lives a long time.

Dochtúir na sláinte an codladh.
Health's doctor is sleep.

Home

Níl aon tinteán mar do thinteán féin.
There's no hearth like your own hearth.

Honesty

Ní dhíolann dearmad fiacha.
A debt is still unpaid, even if forgotten.

Filleann an feall ar an bhfeallaire.
The wrong returns to the wrongdoer.

Human nature

Bíonn gach duine go lách go dtéann bó ina gharraí.
Everybody is good-natured until a cow goes into
   his garden.

DON'T THINK OF IT AS A
BIG SMELLY COW PAT. THINK
OF IT AS MANURE.

Is í ding di féin a scoileann an dair.
It is a wedge of itself that splits the oak.

Is iomaí fear fada a bhíonn lag ina lár.
Many a tall man has a weak middle.

Is minic ubh bhán ag cearc dhubh.
A black hen often has a white egg.

Ní chruinníonn cloch reatha caonach.
A rolling stone gathers no moss.

Ní dhéanfadh an domhan capall rása d'asal.
You can't make a racehorse out of a donkey.

Seachnaíonn súil ní nach bhfeiceann.
What the eye does not see, the heart does not
    grieve over.

Intelligence and Ignorance

An té nach bhfuil láidir, ní mór dó a bheith glic.
He who is weak needs to be clever.

Is trom an t-ualach an t-aineolas.
Ignorance is a heavy burden.

Justice

Ní raibh feall riamh nach fillfeadh.
Evil always returns on the evildoer.

Ní hé an té is fearr a thuileann is mó a fhaigheann.
The most deserving isn't always the best rewarded.

Laziness

Is trom an t-ualach é an leisce.
Laziness is a heavy load.

Chomh díomhaoin le laidhricín píobaire.
As idle as a piper's little finger.

Snathán fada, táilliur falsa.
A long stitch, a lazy tailor.

Ní dhéanfaidh smaoineamh an treabhadh duit.
You'll never plough a field by turning it over in
your mind.

Life

Fiche bliain ag fás, fiche bliain faoi bhláth agus fiche bliain ag trá.
Twenty years a-growing, twenty years in bloom, and twenty years in decline.

Ith do sháith agus ól do sháith agus déan do sháith den obair, agus nuair a gheobhas tú bás, féadfaidh tú do sháith a chodladh.
Eat and drink your fill and work your best, and when you die, you can sleep your rest.

Trí ní nach mothaítear ag teacht: cíos, aois agus féasóg.
Three things that come unawares: rent, age, and beard growth.

OOPS. FORGOT TO SHAVE THIS MORNING.

An rud a ghoilleas ar an gcroí caithfidh an t-súil é a shileas.
What pains the heart must be washed away with tears.

Níl aon suáilce gan a duáilce féin.
There are no unmixed blessings in life.

Is fada an bóthar nach mbíonn casadh ann.
It is a long road that has no turning.

Love and Marriage

Is fearr an troid ná an t-uaigneas.
Better to be fighting than to be lonely.

An té a phósfas an t-airgead, pósfaidh sé óinseach. Imeoidh an t-airgead, fanfaidh an t-óinseach.
He who marries money, marries a fool. The money will go but the fool will remain.

Is folamh fuar teach gan bean.
Empty and cold is the house without a woman.

Galar an grá nach leigheasann luibheanna.
No known herb cures love.

Ceileann searc ainimh's locht.
Love hides blemishes and defects.

Níl leigheas ar an ghrá ach pósadh.
Love's only remedy is marriage.

An áit a bhfuil do chroí is ann a thabharfas do chosa thú.
Where your heart is, your feet will lead you.

Is minic a chealg briathra míne cailín críonna.
Many a prudent girl was led astray with honeyed words.

Más maith leat do cháineadh, pós.
If you like to be criticised, marry.

An té a bhíonn díomhaoin óg, bíonn sé buan críonna.
He who is single in youth, is forever wise.

*Ón lá a bpósfaidh tú beidh do chroí i do bhéal agus do lámh i
    do phóca.*
From the day you marry your heart will be in your mouth
    and your hand in your pocket.

Miserliness

An té is mó a osclaíonn a bhéal is é is lú a osclaíonn a sparán.
He who opens his mouth the most, opens his purse
the least.

Needs

Is fearr beagán cuidithe ná mórán trua.
A little help is better than a lot of sympathy.

Is cuma leis an bhacach cé a líonann a mhála.
The beggar cares little as to who fills his bag.

Ní sheasann sac folamh.
An empty sack won't stand.

Patience

Tig maith mór as moill bheag.
Great good often comes from a short delay.

De réir a chéile a thógtar na caisleáin.
It takes time to build castles.

Is ceirín do gach créacht an fhoighne.
Patience is a poultice for all wounds.

Coimhéad fearg fhear na foighde.
Beware of the anger of a patient man.

Praise

Níor bhris focal maith fiacail riamh.
A good word never broke a tooth.

Reputation

Caill do chlú agus faigh ar ais é, agus ní hé an rud céanna é.
Lose your reputation and you may regain it, but it is
    never the same.

Is fearr rith maith ná droch sheasamh.
A good fleeing is better than a bad standing.

Is fearr clú ná conach.
A good name is better than riches.

Risk

Ní bhíonn bua mór gan contúirt.
There is never a great victory without danger.

Silence

Is binn béal ina thost.
A closed mouth is sweet.

Success

*An té a bhíonn thuas, óltar deoch air, an té a bhíonn thíos
    buailtear cic air.*
He who is successful is saluted with a drink, he who is
    down is kicked.

Temperance

Bíonn blas ar an mbeagán.
A little tastes well.

Oíche aerach is maidin bhrónach.
A lively night and a sad morning.

An rud is annamh is iontach.
Seldom seen is wonderful.

Time

Dá fhada an lá tagann an tráthnóna.
However long the day, the evening will come.

Téann an saol thart mar bheadh eiteoga air agus cuireann gach aon Nollaig bliain eile ar do ghualainn.
Life goes by as if it had wings and every Christmas puts another year on your shoulder.

Ní fhanann trá le fear mall.
The tide does not wait for a slow man.

Is maith an scéalaí an aimsir.
Time is a good storyteller.

Timing

Ní hé lá na gaoithe lá na scoilbe.
A windy day is no day for thatching.

Time-wasting

An rud nach fiú é a lorg, ní fiú é a fháil.
What's not worth seeking, is not worth finding.

Ná bris do loigrín ar stól nach bhfuil i do shlí.
Don't break your shin on a stool that's not in your way.

Togetherness

Ní neart go cur le chéile.
Unity is strength.

Ar scáth a chéile a mhairimid.
We all exist in each others' shadow.

Truth

Ní féidir an dubh a chur ina gheal ach seal.
Black can only be made white for a short while.

Bíonn an fhírinne searbh ach ní fhaigheann sí náire go deo.
Truth is bitter but never ashamed.

Wealth

Bíonn saibhir agus daibhir le chéile ar neamh.
Rich and poor are together in heaven.

Téann íseal agus uasal chuig tórramh.
Both poor and rich attend funerals.

Ní thuigeann an sách an seang.
The well-fed does not understand the lean.

Weather

Dearg aniar: soineann agus grian.
    Red in the west: calm and sunny.
Dearg anoir: sneachta agus sioc.
    Red in the east: snow and frost.
Dearg aneas: doineann agus teas.
    Red in the south: storm and heat.
Dearg aduaidh: clagar agus fuacht.
    Red in the north: hail and cold.

Is garbh mí na gcuach.
The month of the cuckoo is severe.

Teas gaoithe aduaidh nó fuacht gaoithe aneas, sin báisteach.
A warm north wind or a cold south wind means rain.

Wisdom

Níl saoi gan locht.
There's no wise man
    without fault.

*Is ón cheann a thagann
    an cheird.*
The craft comes from
    the head.

Is leor nod don eolach.
A hint is sufficient for the wise.

EH MICK, I THINK YOU FORGOT TO PUT YOUR TROUSERS ON THIS MORNING.

THERE'S NO WISE MAN WITHOUT FAULT.

Women

Is foisge do bhean leithsgéal ná bráiscin!
A woman has an excuse readier than an apron!

Trí shaghas fear nach féidir leo mná a thuiscint: fir óga, fir aosta agus fir mheánaosta.
Three types of men who don't understand women: young men, old men, and middle-aged.

Ná glac pioc comhairle gan comhairle ban.
Never take advice without a woman's guidance.

An áit a mbíonn mná bíonn caint agus an áit a mbíonn géanna bíonn callán.
Where there are women there is talk and where there are geese there is cackling.

Trí ní is deacair a thuiscint; intleacht na mban, obair na mbeach, teacht agus imeacht na taoide.
Three things hard to understand; the intellect of women, the work of bees, the coming and going of the tide.

Work

Molann an obair an fear.
The work praises the man.

Is geall le sos malairt oibre.
A change is as good as a rest.

Is deas an rud an beagán ach é a dhéanamh go maith.
Little is best if well done.

Déan an fál nó iocfaidh tú foghail.
Make the fence or you will pay the plundering.

DAMN. THEY MADE A FENCE. THERE'LL BE NO THIEVIN' TODAY.

Ní breac go port é.
A trout isn't caught until landed.

An t-ualach 's mó ar an capall is míne.
The willing horse gets the most work.

An té nach gcuireann san earrach, ní bhainfidh sé san fhómhair.
He who does not sow in spring will not reap in autumn.

Tús maith leath na hoibre.
A good beginning is half the work.

Imíonn an tuirse ach fanann an tairbhe.
The tiredness leaves but the profit remains.

Luigh leis an uan, agus éirigh leis an éan.
Go to sleep with the lamb, and rise with the bird.

Is fearr lán doirn de cheird ná lán mála d'ór.
A handful of skill is better than a bagful of gold.

Is crua a cheannaíonn an droim an bolg.
The back must slave to feed the belly.

Ní hiad na fir mhóra a bhaineas an fomhar i gcónaí.
It is not always the great men that reap the harvest.

Youth

Ná cuir dailtín le teachtaireacht.
Never send a youngster with a message.

Is cuma leis an óige cá leagann sí a cos.
Youth does not mind where it sets its foot.

Bíonn ceann caol ar an óige.
You cannot put an old head on the young.

glossary

Athlone

Town that lies on the River Shannon in the midlands of Ireland.

Black and Tans

Men recruited by the Royal Irish Constabulary to suppress revolution in Ireland.

Book of Kells

Heavily illustrated book containing the four Gospels of the New Testament, created by Irish monks around 800.

Croke Park/Croker

The main athletic stadium of Ireland.

Curragh

Ireland's premier horse racecourse, is located on this large plain in Co. Kildare.

Daíl

Lower house of the Irish Parliament.

Gaelic Athletic Association (GAA)

Irish sporting and cultural organization that promotes traditional Irish sports, including hurling, camogie, Gaelic football, handball, and rounders.

Garda

Short name for the Irish police force.

Daniel O'Connell (1775–1847)

Irish political leader who campaigned for Catholic Emancipation and the repeal of the Act of Union.

Shillelagh

A village located in Co. Wicklow in southeastern Ireland.

Spoonerism

A type of error in speech where sounds are switched.

Taoiseach

The head of government of Ireland.

Workhouse

A place where people unable to support themselves went to live and work. Conditions were generally terrible and abusive.

índex